A nostalgic look at

LLANDUDNO AND COLWYN BAY TRAMS

Since 1945

Geoff Price

Silver Link Publishing Ltd

THE LLANDUDNO & COLWYN BAY ELECTRIC RAILWAY LTD.

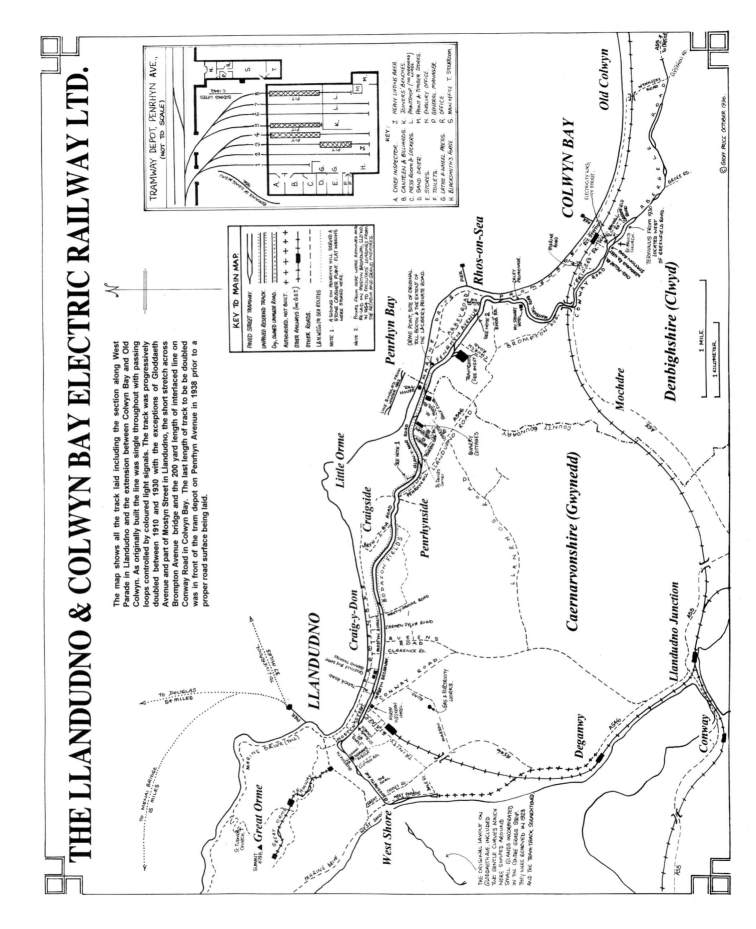

The map shows all the track laid including the section along West Parade in Llandudno and the extension between Colwyn Bay and Old Colwyn. As originally built the line was single throughout with passing loops controlled by coloured light signals. The track was progressively doubled between 1910 and 1930 with the exceptions of Gloddaeth Avenue and part of Mostyn Street in Llandudno, the short stretch across Brompton Avenue bridge and the 200 yard length of interlaced line on Conway Road in Colwyn Bay. The last length of track to be be doubled was in front of the tram depot on Penrhyn Avenue in 1938 prior to a proper road surface being laid.

KEY TO MAIN MAP.

PRIVED STREET TRAMWAY.

UNNAMED RESERVED TRACK.

Oq, OWNED UNMADE ROAD.

AUTHORISED, NOT BUILT.

OTHER RAILWAYS (inc G.O.T.)

OTHER ROADS.

LLANW & CLUB SEA ROUTES . . . .

NOTE 1. A SIDING ON PENRHYN HILL SERVED A STONE CRUSHER PLANT. FLAT WAGONS WERE STORED HERE.

NOTE 2. POINTS FROM HERE WERE REMOVED AND RE-LAID ON MOSTYN BROADBANK, LLOYD IN 1934 TO FACILITATE LOADING/UNLOADING FROM THE ARCADIA AND GRAND THEATRES.

TRAMWAY DEPOT, PENRHYN AVE.
(NOT TO SCALE)

SIDING LIFTED C.1942.

KEY:
A. CHIEF INSPECTOR.
B. CANTEEN & BILLIARDS.
C. MESS ROOM & LOCKERS.
D. SAND DRIER.
E. STOKERS.
F. TOILETS.
G. LATHE & WHEEL PRESS.
H. BLACKSMITH'S FORGE.
J. HEAVY LIFTING AREA.
K. JOINERS' BENCHES.
L. PAINTSHOP (No OVERSHOW) & UNSEE.
M. PAINT & TIMBER STORES.
N. EXBURY OFFICE.
P. GENERAL MANAGER.
R. OFFICE.
S. MAIN OFFICE T. STOCKROOM

© GEOF. PRICE OCTOBER 1996.

To MENAI BRIDGE
15 MILES

St. TUDNO'S
CHURCH

SUMMIT
679ft. ▲ Great Orme

GREAT ORME

MARINE DRIVE (TOLL)

To LIVERPOOL
37 MILES

To DOUGLAS
51 MILES

LLANDUDNO

Little Orme

Craigside

Penrhynside

Craig-y-Don

BODAFON FIELDS

Penrhyn Bay

ORME POINT, SITE OF ORIGINAL TOLL BOOTH & THE EXTENT OF THE L&C&BE'S PRIVATE ROAD.

PIER

Rhos-on-Sea

MARINE ROAD

ELECTRICITY WKS. IVY STREET.

COLWYN BAY

Old Colwyn

WYNNSTAY ROAD

A547

GROES RD.

A55 TO CHESTER

GLYDDFAEN RD.

TERMINUS FROM 1930 LOCATED WEST OF GREENFIELD ROAD.

Mochdre

Denbighshire (Clwyd)

A547

COUNTY BOUNDARY

1 MILE.

1 KILOMETER.

Caernarvonshire (Gwynedd)

Llandudno Junction

Deganwy

A546

A55

Conway

West Shore

THE ORIGINAL LAYOUT ON GLODDAETH AVE. INCLUDED TWO GENTLE CURVES WHICH WERE SHAPED AROUND SMALL ISLANDS INCORPORATED IN THE CENTRE GRASS STRIP. THEY WERE REMOVED IN 1923 AND THE TRAM TRACK STRAIGHTENED.

CONTENTS

Foreword by Terry Jones 5

Introduction 7
A brief history of the Llandudno and Colwyn Bay
tramway 9
Llandudno and Colwyn Bay trams in colour 26
Fleet summary 28

To Colwyn Bay 34

Tramway miscellany 68
To Llandudno 82
The last day 113
The steamers 123
The Great Orme Railway 126
Rhyl miniature tramway 129
Postscript 131

Index 132

The interior of tram No 2 taken during the summer of 1955 as the car travels along Penrhyn Avenue. Conductor Bob Morgan can be seen issuing tickets while the passengers, mostly locals, chat to each other or gaze out of the windows at the passing scene. The upholstered seat cushions acquired from redundant Birmingham trams in 1953 can also be seen. *Eric Cope*

© Geoffrey W. Price 1997

All rights reserved. No part of this publication may be reproduced, stored in a retrieval system or transmitted, in any form or by any means, electronic, mechanical, photocopying, recording or otherwise, without prior permission in writing from Silver Link Publishing Ltd.

First published in June 1997

British Library Cataloguing in Publication Data

A catalogue record for this book is available from the British Library.

ISBN 1 85794 094 6

Silver Link Publishing Ltd
Unit 5, Home Farm Close
Church Street, Wadenhoe
Peterborough PE8 5TE
Tel (01832) 720440
Fax (01832) 720531
e-mail: pete@slinkp-p.demon.co.uk

Printed and bound in Great Britain

ACKNOWLEDGEMENTS

BEING PARTICULARLY interested in this tramway, I have gathered, and still require, information, photographs and the loan of documents relating to all aspects of its operation, which will eventually enable me to prepare my fully comprehensive history of the line.

In this respect, to date a number of people have been most helpful to me and I acknowledge their valued contributions here. Without their assistance, this particular project might not have been possible. They are: Roy Anderson, Richard Allen, Joe Bellamy, Roger Best, Vic Bradley, Roy Brook, Arthur Button, Denis Butler, Peter Caldwell, Geoffrey Claydon, Eric Cope, Jim Copland, Neil Crewdson, Godfrey Croughton, Susan Ellis, Philip Evans, John Fozard, Ted Gahan, Mike Goodwyn, E. C. Haywood, Philip Groves, Jim Halsall, Martin Jenkins, D. W. K. Jones, John Glyn Jones, Greg Lawson, Geoff Leigh, Stan Letts, Vernon Linden, Geoff Lord, Brian Martin, Ken Mansell, George Mather, Mike Mercer, Harry Moore, Roy Marshall, Bernard Norgate, George Oakley, Eric Old, Owen Prosser, Henry Priestley, Stuart and Elan Rivers, Ken Swallow, John Symons, Keith Terry, Eric Thornton, Fred Ward, Roger Webster, Ron White of Colour-Rail, Richard Wiseman and Fred Woolley.

Particular thanks must go to Rosie Thacker and Glyn Wilton of the National Tramway Museum at Crich, Derbyshire, for access to information and for printing a considerable number of photographs held in their vast collection. Their permission for these pictures to be reproduced here is gratefully acknowledged. (I have abbreviated the copyright credit, where applicable, to NTM.) Readers not familiar with tramcars would be well advised to visit the splendid Museum to find out more about our tramway heritage.

Special thanks must also go to David Packer for supplying prints from his extensive range of tramway negatives and for his generosity in allowing them to be used in this album.

Each photograph has been credited in the appropriate caption where the photographer's name is known. Where it has not been possible to identify the source of any print, this has also been noted, and my apologies in advance to any photographer whose work has been used without proper acknowledgement.

My personal thanks to Paul and Wendy Gardener for the loan of their computer to deal with my manuscript, and to Clive Slade and Sue Walker for sorting out all the problems encountered while trying to master the infernal machine! Also to editor Will Adams and Silver Link Publishing for agreeing to include this system in their expanding range of 'A nostalgic look at. . .' tramway albums.

And finally, the biggest 'thank you' for years of patience, tolerance, understanding and good humour to my wife June and daughters Gillian, Claire, Emma and Alison, to whom this album is dedicated.

BIBLIOGRAPHY

Aaron, Henry *Street Furniture* (Shire Publications Ltd, 2nd ed, 1987)

Anderson, R. C. *A History of Crosville Motor Services* (David & Charles, 1981)
A History of the Llandudno & Colwyn Bay Electric Railway Limited (Quail Map Co, 1968)
Great Orme Railway (Light Railway Transport League)

Crosland-Taylor, W. J. *State Owned Without Tears* (Littlebury Bros, 1954)

Duckworth, C. L. D., and Langmuir, G. E. *West Coast Steamers* (Stephenson & Sons, 1953)

Edwards, G. *Colwyn Bay, a Social History 1934-1984* (Colwyn Borough Council, 1984)

Jones, Ivor Wynn *Colwyn Bay, a Brief History* (Clwyd Library Service, 1995)
Llandudno, Queen of the Welsh Resorts (John Jones Cardiff Ltd, 1975)

Lawson, R., and Morris, G. C. J. *The Llandudno & Colwyn Bay Electric Railway* (Light Railway Transport League, 1956)

Martin, Brian P. *Trams, a Nostalgic Look Back* (Llandudno Tramway Society)

Price, Geoff *Trams Leave Here for Llandudno & Colwyn Bay* (Pride Books, 1982)

Senior, Michael *Llandudno's Story* (Gwasg Carreg Gwalch, 1986)

Thornley, F. C. *Past and Present Steamers of North Wales* (Stephenson & Sons, 1962)

Tucker, N. *Colwyn Bay: Its Origin and Growth* (Colwyn Bay Borough Council, 1953)

Turner, Keith *North Wales Tramways* (David & Charles, 1979)
The Llandudno and Colwyn Bay Electric Railway (Oakwood Press, 1993)

Other sources include relevant local newspapers and periodicals, trade press, County Archives of Clwyd and Gwynedd, Light Railway Orders, Ordnance Survey maps, back numbers of *Modern Tramway* and *Tramway Review*, personal correspondence and a host of assorted items relating to the L&CBER.

FOREWORD

Terry Jones

WHEN MY FATHER was serving with the RAF in India during the Second World War, he and some friends went up into the hills above Delhi (as I remember the story) to spend a day's leave in a small village. Back in North Wales he had left behind his wife, his three-year-old son Nigel, and me, six months. We were living in a house called 'Bod Hwyl' in the Dolwyn Road, Old Colwyn. My father must have felt as remote and far away from his new family as any man has ever felt in his life. But as he and his mates sat by the unfamiliar roadside drinking tea, somebody murmured, 'Oh look!', and my father looked up to see a bus coming down the dusty road. It was a bus or charabanc just like the ones that still drove around Colwyn Bay and Llandudno, and there on its destination board was a sign that read 'To Old Colwyn and Dolwyn'.

For a brief moment my father felt that he could jump aboard and be home with his family in time for tea. Then the reality sank in. He was still in the hills above Delhi, in the middle of a war that would go on for who knew how long, and by the time he returned to the Dolwyn Road everything would have changed, his wife four years older, his children unrecognisable.

I feel a little like he must have felt then when I look at the photos in this book of Llandudno and Colwyn Bay trams. Something I thought was far way is suddenly brought right here and present. And yet the realisation soon sets in that it was all a long time ago and will never be the same.

The clank and rattle of those trams, which so terrified me as a small child being pushed on board by my mother, has receded beyond the horizon of sound. Those driving handles, which so mesmerised me as the tram driver started and stopped his tram, I now only see turning on the hall lights in Terry Gilliam's house in London. And yet the excitement of those wonderful vehicles is still here inside me. There was an awkward magic about how they transported you around, being neither train nor bus - they moved in some other way that was definable only as 'tramminess'. The clank and clatter and jerk produced an oddly smooth ride - out of the chaos came order. Magical ordinariness.

Those trams also represented the very idea of public transport. As they scooted along the Abergele Road or past the shops in the Conway Road, across the open bits of country and around the few private cars and lorries, they were a benign presence that meant easy, cheap transportation through a familiar world. Nowadays the private car has driven all before it, and the price has been a swathe cut through the heart of Colwyn Bay. At the time when the photos in this book were taken, the Prom and the sea-front were cut off from the town by the railway; now they are even further cut off by a four-lane motorway roaring its head off through the very centre. The town has been raped by private transport. Perhaps the tram will return, but the town will never be the same again. . .

LLANDUDNO & COLWYN BAY
TRAMS
ELECTRIC RAILWAY LTD.

SUMMER FARES & STAGES
30th May to 11th September, inclusive

WEST BOUND TOWARDS LLANDUDNO

Stage No.

2d.
1. Colwyn Bay (Greenfield Road) and Everard Road.
2. Marine Road (Odeon) and Rhos Road.
3. Everard Road and Penrhyn Drive.
4. Rhos Road and Penrhyn Bay (Maesgwyn Road).
5. Church Road and Little Orme Cafe.
6. Penrhyn Bay (Maesgwyn Road) and Bryn-y-Bia Road.
7. Little Orme Cafe and Nant-y-Gamar Road.
8. Penrhynside and Queen's Road.
9. Nant-y-Gamar Road and Palladium.
10. North Western Hotel and West Shore.

3d.
1. Colwyn Bay (Greenfield Road) and Rhos Road.
2. Marine Road (Odeon) and Penrhyn Drive.
3. Everard Road and Penrhyn Bay (Maesgwyn Road).
4. Rhos Road and Little Orme Cafe.
5. Church Road and Bryn-y-Bia Road.
6. Penrhyn Bay (Maesgwyn Road) and Nant-y-Gamar Road.
7. Penrhynside and North Western Hotel.
8. Bryn-y-Bia Road and Palladium.
9. Nant-y-Gamar Road and West Shore.

4d.
1. Colwyn Bay (Greenfield Road) and Penrhyn Drive.
2. Marine Road (Odeon) and Penrhyn Bay (Maesgwyn Road).
3. Everard Road and Little Orme Cafe.
4. Rhos Road and Bryn-y-Bia Road.
5. Church Road and Nant-y-Gamar Road.
6. Penrhyn Bay (Maesgwyn Road) and Queen's Road.
7. Little Orme Cafe and Palladium.
8. Bryn-y-Bia Road and West Shore.

5d.
1. Colwyn Bay (Greenfield Rd.) and Penrhyn Bay (Maesgwyn Rd.)
2. Marine Road (Odeon) and Little Orme Cafe.
3. Everard Road and Bryn-y-Bia Road.
4. Rhos Road and Nant-y-Gamar Road.
5. Church Road and Queen's Road.
6. Penrhyn Bay (Maesgwyn Road) and Palladium.
7. Little Orme Cafe and West Shore.

6d.
1. Colwyn Bay (Greenfield Road) and Penrhynside.
2. Marine Road (Odeon) and Bryn-y-Bia Road.
3. Everard Road and Nant-y-Gamar Road.
4. Rhos Road and North Western Hotel.
5. Church Road and Palladium.
6. Penrhyn Bay (Maesgwyn Road) and West Shore.

7d.
1. Colwyn Bay (Greenfield Road) and Nant-y-Gamar Road.
2. Marine Road (Odeon) and North Western Hotel.
3. Everard Road and Palladium.
4. Rhos Road and West Shore.

8d.
1. Colwyn Bay (Greenfield Road) and North Western Hotel.
2. Marine Road (Odeon) and Palladium.
3. Everard Road and West Shore.

9d.
1. Colwyn Bay (Greenfield Road) and Palladium or West Shore.

EAST BOUND TOWARDS COLWYN BAY

Stage No.

2d.
10. West Shore and North Western Hotel.
9. Palladium and Nant-y-Gamar Road.
8. Queen's Road and Penrhynside.
7. Nant-y-Gamar Road and Little Orme Cafe.
6. Bryn-y-Bia Road and Penrhyn Bay (Maesgwyn Road).
5. Little Orme Cafe and Church Road.
4. Penrhyn Bay (Maesgwyn Road) and Rhos Road.
3. Penrhyn Drive and Everard Road.
2. Rhos Road and Marine Road (Odeon).
1. Everard Road and Colwyn Bay (Greenfield Road).

3d.
9. West Shore and Nant-y-Gamar Road.
8. Palladium and Bryn-y-Bia Road.
7. North Western Hotel and Penrhynside.
6. Nant-y-Gamar Road and Penrhyn Bay (Maesgwyn Road).
5. Bryn-y-Bia Road and Church Road.
4. Little Orme Cafe and Rhos Road.
3. Penrhyn Bay (Maesgwyn Road) and Everard Road.
2. Penrhyn Drive and Marine Road (Odeon).
1. Rhos Road and Colwyn Bay (Greenfield Road).

4d.
8. West Shore and Bryn-y-Bia Road.
7. Palladium and Little Orme Cafe.
6. Queen's Road and Penrhyn Bay (Maesgwyn Road).
5. Nant-y-Gamar Road and Church Road.
4. Bryn-y-Bia Road and Rhos Road.
3. Little Orme Cafe and Everard Road.
2. Penrhyn Bay (Maesgwyn Road) and Marine Road (Odeon).
1. Penrhyn Drive and Colwyn Bay (Greenfield Road).

5d.
7. West Shore and Little Orme Cafe.
6. Palladium and Penrhyn Bay (Maesgwyn Road).
5. Queen's Road and Church Road.
4. Nant-y-Gamar Road and Rhos Road.
3. Bryn-y-Bia Road and Everard Road.
2. Little Orme Cafe and Marine Road (Odeon).
1. Penrhyn Bay (Maesgwyn Rd.) and Colwyn Bay (Greenfield Rd.)

6d.
6. West Shore and Penrhyn Bay (Maesgwyn Road).
5. Palladium and Church Road.
4. North Western Hotel and Rhos Road.
3. Nant-y-Gamar Road and Everard Road.
2. Bryn-y-Bia Road and Marine Road (Odeon).
1. Penrhynside and Colwyn Bay (Greenfield Road).

7d.
4. West Shore and Rhos Road.
3. Palladium and Everard Road.
2. North Western Hotel and Marine Road (Odeon).
1. Nant-y-Gamar Road and Colwyn Bay (Greenfield Road).

8d.
3. West Shore and Everard Road.
2. Palladium and Marine Road (Odeon).
1. North Western Hotel and Colwyn Bay (Greenfield Road).

9d.
1. West Shore or Palladium and Colwyn Bay (Greenfield Road).

CHILDREN UNDER 14 YEARS OF AGE, HALF SINGLE FARE (FRACTIONS OF 1d. BEING RECKONED AS 1d.). INFANTS IN ARMS UNDER 3 YEARS OF AGE AND NOT OCCUPYING A SEAT, FREE.

WORKERS' DAY RETURN TICKETS ARE ISSUED BEFORE 9 a.m. ON ANY ORDINARY 2d. STAGE AND OVER, AT SINGLE FARE FOR RETURN JOURNEY, SUBJECT TO THE FIRST JOURNEY EACH DAY BEING COMPLETED BEFORE 9 a.m.

Tramway Depot,
Rhos-on-Sea.
May, 1954.

H. T. JONES,
Assistant Manager.

POWLSONS, THE COLWYN BAY PRESS

INTRODUCTION

MY FATHER'S FAMILY had taken their summer holidays in Llandudno for many years. The town was full of happy memories for them, so it was only natural for the pattern to continue. My family enjoyed holidays there every year throughout my childhood. My love of trams began at 9 months of age when I saw a Llandudno tram for the first time! I can recall the great wave of excitement and anticipation that I felt sitting in the back seat of our motor car as we approached Colwyn Bay, hoping that there would be a tram standing at its terminus. For me, seeing the trams there again meant that the holiday had really started.

Travelling towards Llandudno our route followed the busy A55 through Colwyn Bay to Brompton Avenue railway bridge, where we then followed the A546 to Llandudno and reached the foot of the Little Orme. This was a particularly steep hill and the tramway was built on a shelf of the hillside above the roadway. At the top of the hill two tall poles carried the message 'Llandudno Welcomes You' slung between them on cables and illuminated at night with tungsten bulbs. Crossing the tram tracks the road swept gently away over the neck of the Little Orme to reveal the town of Llandudno laid out in front of us. The magnificent bay with its wide promenade flanked by large, well-kept hotels and boarding houses drew the viewer's eye to the Great Orme, that large carboniferous limestone headland that dominates the scene and provides the town with its magnificent backdrop.

As our motor car descended from the Little Orme to the promenade I would look first to the left to see if there was any sign of a tram moving through the fields, then towards the sea with its waves breaking on to the shingle beach. Having arrived at our hotel I wanted to be out and about, but was forced to wait until things had been unpacked and put away. If the day was fine, some time would be spent on the beach, but whatever the weather the tramride to Colwyn Bay and back was obligatory and took place a few times during the week-long holiday.

Invariably after dinner I would be taken to see Professor Codman's evening performance of Punch and Judy. This took place near the entrance to the Pier and was always a popular feature of the town during the summer holiday periods. Other childhood memories include driving the motorboats on the pool situated immediately behind the entrance to the pier, and being taken on the Great Orme tram to the half-way station, then walking over to either the Pink farm or the White farm for a lemonade and a cake before continuing on over the top of the hill and down into the Happy Valley.

I recall on a visit to Colwyn Bay standing in the doorway of a shop in Abergele Road and seeing what looked like a brand new streamlined tram glide up the rise towards the terminus. Its paintwork was very clean and it had a brand new white trolley rope. As my mother's interest in the shops prolonged our visit, the new tram

had departed and our journey back to Llandudno was made on one of the original trams that dated from 1907.

On two occasions during the 1950s I was taken to Llandudno by boat from Liverpool on board the TSS *St Tudno* operated by the Liverpool & North Wales Steamship Co Ltd. The approach to the town by sea was an interesting experience. Due to the fact that the town was built on the low-lying flat land between the two Ormes, the Great Orme at first appeared to be an island, the larger buildings in the town not becoming visible until the ship was about 3 miles out from the pier.

Upon disembarking from the vessel at Llandudno Pier, a walk was taken to the Happy Valley and up past the little theatre on to a knoll called Camera Hill, where there was a wooden hut that contained a camera obscura. In the darkened room was a circular white table that acted as a screen, and images outside were projected by mirrors and lenses from a turret on the top of the roof. I recall being amazed to see the image of the bay and the town on the table in front of me . . . and in colour too!

After 1953 we did not holiday in the town again as a family, but in 1954, on a day visit by motor car, I wanted to ride on the tram to Colwyn Bay and back. My parents waited with me at the tram stop at Palladium Corner and one of the famous 'toast-rack' trams arrived from the West Shore. I climbed on board alongside the conductor, facing to the rear, and my father asked him to keep an eye on me. The round trip was approximately 80 minutes. It was the first and only occasion I rode on one of these trams. It was a glorious afternoon and the journey to Colwyn Bay and back was all the more memorable because of the very fast ride down Bryn-y-Bia Road and the Bodafon fields.

On Wednesday evening, 14 March 1956, I returned home from the weekly Boy Scout meeting to be greeted by my mother and father with some bad news. They showed me an article in that evening's *Liverpool Echo* headed 'Llandudno Losing its Trams'. The trams were due to finish a week from the following Saturday, and as my father always worked on Saturdays a trip by car was out of the question. Mother, realising how much I wanted to be there, telephoned a friend and asked if her son, David, would like to accompany me on the trip to North Wales. Luckily for me he agreed and we met at Liverpool Pier Head to board the Crosville Express bus for Llandudno on the morning of Saturday 24 March.

We arrived in Llandudno at lunch time, ate our sandwiches quickly and stood at the Palladium Corner tram stop. Presently a tram arrived on 'Special Car' duty and proceeded towards West Shore. Another tram arrived from the Colwyn Bay direction and stopped to let its passengers off, many carrying cameras. Just then our tram arrived from West Shore, an open-top double-decker. First in the queue, we climbed the stairs and made for the front seat next to the upper-deck light. The tram soon filled up and the conductor, who was now on the top deck, blew his whistle and the tram moved off into Mostyn Street.

Being March, the ride was far colder than in summer, but we were both well wrapped up. The day was bright although the sun had not penetrated the mist, and travelling across the Bodafon Fields we began to feel the goose pimples on our legs! As the tram climbed passed the Craigside halt, I remember looking back towards Llandudno, finding it very difficult to imagine that within a few hours the trams would be just a memory.

We travelled through to Colwyn Bay terminus and remained with the tram until it reached the tramsheds at Rhos-on-Sea, where we alighted and joined dozens of other people in the depot yard clambering on all of the trams there. In the middle of our explorations a tram came into the depot yard having broken something underneath; another tram was moved out on to Penrhyn Avenue to replace it. We resumed our explorations until David said that we needed to be thinking of getting back to Llandudno in time to get the bus home.

Presently the double-deck tram that had replaced the disabled one arrived from Colwyn Bay and we boarded her at the Church Road stop. We rode back to Llandudno on the top deck just as the sun finally broke through the mist. At the West Shore terminus most of the passengers got off to take photographs, but David and I remained in our seats. The tram moved off again, along Gloddaeth Avenue and eventually arrived at Palladium Corner, where another long queue of people waited to board. We rode as far as the North Western Hotel on Mostyn Street and alighted. The tram pulled away from us and, with the distinctive clatter over short rail joints, accelerated along Mostyn Broadway towards Craig-y-Don.

We walked around the corner into Conway Road and waited for the bus to Liverpool. As we stood there, another tram came into view on Mostyn Broadway heading into Llandudno. Our bus arrived and we departed from Llandudno, looking out for a glimpse of a tram where we passed along the tram route.

As we reached the Crosville Office on Conway Road at Colwyn Bay, I looked back along Conway Road and there, bathed in the last golden rays of a watery sun, was the tram from which we had alighted in Llandudno, her lights twinkling in the twilight as she rolled gently into Colwyn Bay. That was the last time I was to see the trams that were so much a part of my early life.

The intervening years have been kind to Llandudno. Although there has been development of housing and both new and re-development of parts of the centre, the town retains much of its charm and character and is a vibrant centre for shopping all the year round. It can be as difficult to find an on-street car parking space in January as it is in August. The hoteliers and boarding house keepers appear to have adjusted well to the changing habits and requirements of the British holidaymaker.

It is still possible to feel and hear the hollow crunching sound as you walk along the shingle beach, to wander around on the Great Orme in search of the wild goats and to hear the call of the seagulls as they circle almost continuously over the town. The donkeys still ply their trade on the beach during the summer and Mr Punch is no nearer sorting out his family problems than he was 50 years ago! Visitors to the town today can now explore the Copper Mines on the Orme, and it is even possible to follow Alice and the White Rabbit down that most famous of rabbit holes created in Llandudno by Lewis Carroll. Although what Alice might think of the prospect of being able to ski or toboggan all the year round on the Great Orme, one can only guess!

People who know and love the North Wales coast and Llandudno in particular will undoubtedly have their own favourite memories of the area. I am fortunate to be able to share some of mine with you thanks largely to a publisher who has had the vision to produce a series of similar albums featuring scenes within living memory for those of us who are upwards of 50 years of age. Many younger readers will, no doubt, be amazed at the apparent lack of traffic in many of the photographs, and yet during the period covered by this album, it was already becoming a problem. Television was beginning to make great strides forward, and as the 1950s gave way to a new decade progress generally was going to accelerate faster than most people could imagine.

With the pace of life today I sometimes wonder if our children will look back on their own childhood with affection. I certainly hope so, and if they can return to a place as adults that has remained basically unchanged from the way that they remember it, then they will indeed be fortunate. Each time I cross over the Little Orme and look down upon Llandudno I feel as if I have returned home and, for a few hours at least, can recapture some elements of earlier days when I didn't have a care in the world.

A BRIEF HISTORY OF THE LLANDUDNO AND COLWYN BAY TRAMWAY

AS THE 19TH CENTURY drew to a close, the towns of Llandudno and Colwyn Bay were expanding rapidly, not only as holiday resorts but also as residential and business centres. Both towns supported a residential population of around 6,500 people, figures that were considerably expanded during the summer months with the large influx of holidaymakers who flocked to the newly developed North Wales coast resorts.

By 1892 the only transport link between the two towns was the railway, and that was somewhat circuitous, via Llandudno Junction and along the branch line through Deganwy to Llandudno, so the possibility of creating a more direct link between Colwyn Bay and Llandudno, embracing Rhos-on-Sea, Penrhyn Bay and Penrhynside attracted the attention of would-be promoters of electric tramway schemes. Between 1892 and 1897 six different proposals were submitted, but failed for various reasons. Their story is beyond the scope of this book, but as a result the district as a whole was made aware of the advantages of a tramway system.

Eventually, following months of protracted wrangling between promoters Light Railway & General Construction Company Limited, local landowner the Hon E. M. L. Mostyn MP and the Llandudno Urban District Council, with concessions being given and conditions being met (the UDC dropped its own limited scheme in favour of the company proposal), the Llandudno & Colwyn Bay Light Railway Order 1898 was confirmed by the Board of Trade on 2 June 1899. This Instrument formed the basis for the creation of an electric tramway that would extend from Colwyn Bay through Rhos-on-Sea, Penrhyn Bay, over the Little Orme and through the centre of Llandudno, eventually terminating opposite the railway station in Deganwy.

The years between 1899 and 1906 are littered with sagas of raising capital and extending time to complete construction to such an extent that no physical signs of work could be seen. Monies raised, it seemed, were being wasted on the legal necessities, and no progress was possible. A change of Company in 1902 saw an application by the Llandudno, Colwyn Bay & Rhyl Electric Traction Co Ltd for an extension of time to raise yet more funds. The Board of Trade confirmed the Llandudno & Colwyn Bay Light Railway (Deviation and Amendment) Order 1903, which included revisions in the route towards Colwyn Bay, on 26 September 1903. Although at this point in time all lands required between Rhos-on-Sea and West Parade, Llandudno, had been purchased, the route from Rhos-on-Sea to Colwyn Bay had not been agreed to the satisfaction of all interested parties, and

negotiations continued. One assumes that the inclusion of the word 'Rhyl' in the title was intended to attract a wider source of investment, for there appears to be no evidence to suggest any intention to extend the line along the coast to that town (it would have been a grossly wasteful duplication of already adequate railway services along the coast between Chester and Holyhead).

By June 1904, following another company title change to the Llandudno & Colwyn Bay Electric Traction Co Ltd, the trade press reported that good progress had been made in construction of the new light railway. In fact, only about 365 yards had been laid! As the completion deadline had expired on 2 June, application was again made to the Board of Trade for yet another extension of time. Despite fresh capital being injected by a London-based Tramways Extension Syndicate, which persuaded the BOT to grant the time extension, it came as no surprise to local people that nothing was happening on the ground. Things were seemingly trapped in the proverbial vicious circle.

The stalemate was ended when the L&CBET Co Ltd went into liquidation in 1906. In July of that year the Llandudno & District Electric Traction Construction Co Ltd was formed jointly with the well-known firm Bruce, Peebles & Co Ltd of Edinburgh to take over the existing powers to construct, open and operate the tramway. By comparison to the 'progress' of the previous seven years, work began early in 1907 and proceeded at a great pace, so much so that the line between Rhos-on-Sea and West Parade, Llandudno, was ready for inspection by the Board of Trade at the end of July.

Part of the new line was built on a privately owned stretch of roadway behind the sea wall in Penrhyn Bay. A 'budget', or toll gate, had existed for a few years near what is now the junction of Marine Drive and Penrhyn Avenue, known as Orme Point. The tram company eventually bought the road from the owner, W. Horton Esq, in 1911 and built a new toll house and gate opposite the entrance to the Rhos-on-Sea Golf Club.

The Board of Trade Inspection was carried out on 9 August 1907, but the Inspector delayed issuing the Certificate to Carry Passengers until all the trams had been fitted with hand-operated brakes in addition to the Westinghouse brakes already incorporated on the cars.

A large eight-road depot was erected on a 1.24-acre site in an area formerly known as 'Klondike' (due to its isolation). In addition to providing covered accommodation for 20 cars, there was a fully equipped workshop, together with routine maintenance and administrative facilities. As originally built, the depot was fitted with eight roller-shutter doors.

Re-inspection took place on 26 September 1907 by Lieut Col Von Donop, who found the trams to be satisfactory. Press advertisements announced that the opening for passenger service would take place on Saturday 19 October, with a half-hourly service commencing at 9 am simultaneously from both ends of the line. The through fare from Rhos-on-Sea (from the junction of what is now Colwyn Avenue/Penrhyn Avenue) to Llandudno terminus, was 5d. From 12 noon until 10.30 pm the service increased to every 15 minutes. Between Rhos-on-Sea and Colwyn Bay a horse bus service was provided by Messrs J. Fred Francis & Sons, Carriage Proprietors of Colwyn Bay, charging a flat fare of 3d. The tramway service and the connection facilities operated Mondays to Saturdays inclusive, no services being operated on Sundays in deference to the strong local feelings for the Sabbath.

It was widely thought that the first public service tram from Llandudno was No 14, and this was probably due to an official postcard view being published of the event. However, reading a contemporary report of a journalist's first ride, and working out the timetable, it would appear that No 14 departed from Rhos-on-Sea at 9 am towards Llandudno, but the identity of the tram that started from Llandudno is not known. There was a stiff north-westerly wind blowing, which was strong enough to dislodge No 14's trolleys from the overhead wires at West Parade and near the foot of the Little Orme. Despite the cold day, crowds packed the trams until the close of service. It is recorded that 4,434 passenger journeys were made on the first day and that a figure in excess of £45 was taken in receipts. (On car 14, 197 fivepenny tickets had been issued between 9 am and 11.25 am.)

As the service began to establish itself, it soon became apparent that the section between Hooson's Corner (the junction of Mostyn Street and Gloddaeth Street, Llandudno) and West Parade was producing very little revenue, so the trams terminated in the centre of Llandudno until the spring, when they operated through to West Parade again. In the early years of the line, the development of the West Shore district of the town was relatively slow and local passenger traffic never amounted to a great deal. The company was to be reminded often during its existence by both local authorities whenever they felt that it was not fulfilling its obligations under the terms of the Light Railway Order, be it operational or maintenance.

Once the tramway was up and running, the company turned its attention to the completion of the Colwyn Bay extension, construction of which had been delayed by local opposition towards the various routes proposed. It had always been the company's intention to try and serve the railway station in Colwyn Bay. Four different proposals for the approach to the town had been made, the route via Brompton Avenue and Conway Road to a temporary terminus at the top of Station Road proving to be the most widely acceptable one. This was approved by the Board of Trade in the Llandudno & Colwyn Bay (Extension and Amendment) Order 1907 on 30 September of that year.

Although this was not quite what the company wanted, the provision for a loop turning off Conway Road, down Penrhyn Road and returning up Station Road to re-join the main route at its junction with Conway and Abergele Roads was inserted but never adopted, and that part of the Order eventually lapsed. The final part of the route stipulated in this Order (between the junction of Station Road and Abergele Road as far as its junction with Groes Road) was not to be completed until the company obtained its powers to extend as far as Old Colwyn.

Services to Colwyn Bay commenced on 7 June 1908, the company having maintained its momentum of getting things done quickly. Eventually the Llandudno & Colwyn Bay Light Railway (Extension No 2) Order 1912 was approved on 1 August of that year, giving approval to extend the line from its temporary terminus in Colwyn Bay, along Abergele Road to the Queens Hotel, Old Colwyn, halfway up the hill leading to Penmaen Head. Construction of this extension was delayed by the track-doubling programme that was proceeding steadily towards Llandudno. It eventually opened for traffic on 26 March 1915, bringing the tramway to its maximum length of 8.14 miles.

Coincidental with a final change of company title in 1909, to the Llandudno & Colwyn Bay Electric Railway Limited, four new tramcars were delivered from the United Electric Car Co Ltd of Preston. These were of unusual semi-convertible design, having enclosed saloons with drop windows, and with additional seats provided on the platforms. Mounted on four-wheel trucks, they quickly earned the nickname 'Yankee' cars due to their decidedly 'non-British' appearance.

From 1909 the track-doubling programme continued towards Llandudno and gradually the tram service improved as each single line obstacle was removed. The route over Penrhyn Hill was widened on the seaward side of the hill, and by 1911 the L&CBER was in negotiation with the Llandudno UDC, which wanted to purchase land owned jointly by the company and W. Horton Esq, to widen and improve the new road to Colwyn Bay at the top of and down Penrhyn Hill. The agreement was that the company sold to the UDC the land it required, and in return the UDC would double the tram track over the newly aligned road junction at the top of the hill and into the start of Bryn-y-Bia Road.

The tram service to the West Shore and West Parade had not produced the returns that would have been liked, and as a result the Duty Inspector would regularly turn trams 'short' at Hooson's Corner, operating through to West Shore during the winter months almost on an 'as required' basis. The UDC was quick to point out that this was not following the terms of the original Order, and sought assurances that things would improve. By 1913, however, the tram company had given up running passenger cars along West Parade, the only journeys being made by one of the 1907 trams pushing a flat wagon along to the dead-end in the sandhills to collect sand for ultimate use in the trams to assist adhesion on steep and wet sections of track.

In July 1914 the views of both Llandudno and Colwyn Bay Councils were sought on the operation of trailer cars or double-decked trams. Both ideas were turned down, Llandudno favouring instead single-deck open tramcars, which it felt would greatly improve the service. In 1915 the company approached the Board of Trade for permis-

Above The only known view of the terminus at the Queens Hotel, Old Colwyn. As ladies in their white summer dresses prepare to board, the conductor has just tied down the trolley at the near end of the tram; the driver will put the other trolley on the wire before changing ends. The narrowness of what is the main coastal road can be plainly seen, and one can only imagine the traffic chaos here in 1930 just prior to the trams being cut back to Colwyn Bay. A major road-widening scheme took place during the 1930s, which caused part of the road towards the top of Penmaen Head to be supported by a bridge; this can be seen today from the A55 Expressway when travelling towards Chester. *NTM*

sion to operate double-deck trams on the route between Rhos-on-Sea and Old Colwyn, having met with strong opposition from Colwyn Bay Council. Permission was given in 1916 following inspection of the route by the BOT, despite the Council's opposition.

In 1914 an order had been placed with the United Electric Car Co for four open 'toast-rack' trams. However, due to the outbreak of the Great War in August, non-essential equipment was deferred until things improved. Consequently the new toast-racks did not arrive until 1920, but when they made their appearance that summer they were an instant hit with the public and their popularity remained undiminished until the end of their last summer in 1955.

The opening of the Old Colwyn section did not save the company from a worsening financial situation, chiefly brought about by shortages of labour, materials and by the general constraints that affected almost all walks of life throughout the country between 1914 and 1918. In July 1920 the company applied to the Ministry of Transport for an Order under the Tramways (Temporary Increase of Charges) Act 1920 to modify the statutory pro-

Right Two pre-1930 'Geographical' tickets (reproduced actual size) showing the Old Colwyn section of the route. *Philip Evans*

A disabled open-top double-deck tram with its trolley tied down off the wire is pushed along Whitehall Road by 'toast-rack' No 19 in the direction of the depot. This was the easiest way to remove the obstruction, although the driver of the toast-rack would have to look through the lower saloon of the tram in front to receive any warnings given by his colleague on the front platform - a different sort of experience for all the passengers concerned.

The driver on toast-rack No 21, Bill Perril, looks as if he has seen it all before as he prepares for the sharp curve leading out into Brompton Avenue. A small boy takes a rest from pushing his wheelbarrow to survey the scene. *Photographer unknown*

visions regulating the charges that the company was authorised to make. (This procedure was available to all tramway undertakings throughout the United Kingdom, and many operators availed themselves of its facilities, the most important of which was to enable fares to be increased.) All relevant facts and figures were presented to a meeting of the Tramway Charges Advisory Committee in London on 16 November 1920 and, following detailed examination of the facts, sanction was given to increase fares in line with the company's requirements. It was also noted that at this time there was still no service on Sundays.

The introduction of the toast-racks had enabled a local service to be re-introduced in Llandudno between the West Shore and Craig-y-Don, operated by the four-wheel 'Yankee' cars much to the delight of local residents who found it particularly difficult to board a tram for a short journey during the main holiday season due to heavy patronage by holidaymakers.

By the late 1920s, traffic had increased considerably along the coastal route and the main road through Colwyn Bay was beginning to feel the strain. Colwyn Bay

UDC introduced a major road improvement scheme to deal with Conway and Abergele Roads, which involved widening and re-surfacing. The tram track was to be doubled concurrent with that work being carried out, the exception being a 200-yard stretch of interlaced track between Coed Pellar Road and Woodland Road West. During the operation the tram service was maintained by having trams serving both sections of the route, passengers having to alight and walk ahead around the roadworks to continue their journey in another tram. While the tracks were severed, trams on the section furthermost from the depot were left in the roadway overnight, the control handles having been removed and their trolleys pulled down under their retaining hooks just in case anyone had ideas about becoming a nocturnal tram driver!

Bus traffic, which had developed rapidly since the end of the war, was giving the tram company a real problem on the Old Colwyn section. The trams could not compete with the newer, faster buses operating the coastal routes. Two problems affecting the company in this matter were the voltage drop at that end of the line due to the fact that the electrical current was still only being fed into the system from Llandudno, and the fact that the original 14 bogie tramcars had their motor capacity reduced from four to two per car, the combined effect causing a loss of power and, consequently, speed where it was most needed.

The tramway company applied to the local Council on 27 March 1930 for licences to operate buses over the Old Colwyn portion of the tram route. It also sought to agree

Fares and Stages, February 1933. *Author's collection*

LLANDUDNO & COLWYN BAY ELECTRIC RLY. LTD.

FARES AND STAGES

1d.

Greenfield Road and Ebberston Road
King's Road and Rhos Post Office
Rhos Post Office and Church Road
Church Road and Penrhyn Bay (Quarry Cottages)
Penrhyn Bay (Quarry Cottages) and Penrhyn Hill
Penrhyn Hill and Nantygamar Road
Bryn-y-bia Road and Queen's Road
Nantygamar Road and St. John's Chapel
Queen's Road and Palladium
St. John's Chapel and Llandudno Terminus

2d.

Greenfield Road and Rhos Post Office
King's Road and Church Road
Rhos Post Office and Penrhyn Bay (Quarry Cottages)
Church Road and Penrhyn Hill
Penrhyn Bay (Quarry Cottages) and Nantygamar Road
Penrhyn Bay (Little Orme Cafe) and Queen's Road
Penrhyn Hill and St. John's Chapel
Bryn-y-bia Road and Palladium
Nantygamar Road and Llandudno Terminus

3d.

Greenfield Road and Church Road
King's Road and Penrhyn Bay (Quarry Cottages)
Rhos Post Office and Penrhyn Hill
Church Road and Nantygamar Road
Penrhyn Bay (Quarry Cottages) and St. John's Chapel
Penrhyn Bay (Little Orme Cafe) and Palladium
Penrhyn Hill and Llandudno Terminus

4d.

Greenfield Road and Penrhyn Bay (Quarry Cottages)
King's Road and Penrhyn Hill
Rhos Post Office and Nantygamar Road
Church Road and St. Johns' Chapel
Penrhyn Bay (Quarry Cottages) and Llandudno Terminus

5d.

Greenfield Road and Penrhyn Hill
King's Road and Nantygamar Road
Rhos Post Office and St. John's Chapel
Church Road and Llandudno Terminus

6d.

Greenfield Road and Nantygamar Road
King's Road and St. John's Chapel
Rhos Post Office and Llandudno Terminus

7d.

Greenfield Road and St. John's Chapel
King's Road and Llandudno Terminus

8d.

Colwyn Bay and Llandudno (Through Fare)

CHILDREN UNDER 14 YEARS OF AGE HALF SINGLE FARES (FRACTIONS OF 1d. BEING RECKONED AS 1d.). INFANTS in ARMS, UNDER 3 YEARS, FREE.

Tramway Depot,
    Rhos-on-Sea.
February, 1933.

W. G. HAMILTON, A.M.I.E.E.,
    General Manager.

Leigh & Williams, Ltd., Printers, Colwyn Bay.

arrangements for the removal of the rails and to obtain assurance from the Council that no other licences would be issued to other bus operators who may compete against the tram company's bus service so long as the public were being adequately served. The Colwyn Bay Council agreed that they would give sympathetic consideration to any further claims the company might have to the granting of any new bus licences.

Early in August the company Chairman, Sir Joseph Nall, wrote to the Council advising them that the L&CBER had acquired an interest in North Wales Silver Motors Ltd, which would operate the buses required to replace the Old Colwyn Trams, and asked for ten omnibus licences, which would be used in conjunction with the 'Silver' licences already held. To compensate passengers in the Old Colwyn area intending to travel through to Llandudno, the L&CBER arranged to run a revised 'Silver' service through to Llandudno alternatively and equally with the Crosville 'Blue' service on a co-ordinated timetable, to which Crosville had also agreed.

One is left wondering what happened to the company's 'interest' in NWSM Ltd, because the latter company was taken over by Crosville on 1 August 1930! It must be reasonably assumed that some form of agreement was entered into between the L&CBER and Crosville to protect the former's interests. The L&CBER did, however, apply for a licence to operate buses over the tram route in an emergency brought about by unforeseen circumstances. A condition attached to the licence stipulated that any buses required would be hired from Crosville.

The possibility of replacing the trams with trolleybuses was aired at this time, but the opinion was that road re-instatement costs involved would outweigh any advantages and the matter was not pursued.

The Old Colwyn tram route was abandoned on Saturday 20 September, Ernie Woolley (later to become an Inspector and Chief Inspector) driving the last tram down from the Queens Hotel. The trams were cut back to St Paul's church until the new terminus was established at the junction with Abergele Road and Greenfield Road. The section of line between Greenfield Road and the Dingle bridge was lifted by direct labour. The remaining rails on the Old Colwyn section were not lifted until 1943 under instruction from the Ministry of Transport.

The siting of the new terminal stub at Greenfield Road caused the police to object to the obstruction caused by trams standing in the centre of the road, so the trams once again used the crossover at St Paul's as the terminus until the road junction on the Greenfield Road side of Abergele Road had been widened and the centre line of the road re-positioned, thereby enabling trams departing for Llandudno to take up their correct position with the general traffic 'flow'.

Sunday running came into operation over the full length of the line at this period, although the trams did not commence until midday, after the recognised church services were over. From 1933 the Sunday operations started earlier at 9 am.

The long-serving manager, Alexander Balfour retired in 1931 and was succeeded by Walter George Hamilton. With the new man came ideas for replacing the original rolling-stock with newer but second-hand trams. The first

An overcast day in August 1951 sees ex-Accrington tram No 2 turning off the promenade at Rhos-on-Sea along Penrhyn Avenue in the direction of Llandudno. A Denbighshire Education Committee van on school meals delivery duty overtakes a Bedford OB coach owned by Messrs Pye's. At the post office an advertising board announces a big fireworks display to be held in Liverpool to celebrate the Festival of Britain (the fireworks were launched from ships in the mouth of the River Mersey between New Brighton and Seaforth and were seen by thousands of people who gathered on both sides of the river and also by invited guests aboard the *St Tudno*).

At the same location in 1996, a rear-engine Bristol double-deck bus (DDM 414V) is operating Crosville service 12 to Rhyl. New development has taken place on the right, and the gap in the buildings seen in the previous picture has also been built up.
H. B. Priestley, NTM/author

of these acquisitions, five single-deck cars with closed saloons and vestibuled platforms, came from the East Lancashire town of Accrington in 1933. Two were complete, although their bogies were re-gauged from 4 ft 0 in to 3 ft 6 in, while the other three bodies were mounted on bogies from the cars that they displaced at Llandudno. Initially they entered service in their Accrington livery but with the L&CBER crest and legal lettering firmly in place.

The same year Colwyn Bay power station in Ivy Street began to produce traction current, and this was fed into the overhead system at St Paul's church and at intervals along the line to the County Boundary on the company's private toll road at Penrhyn Bay.

The next and largest second-hand purchase was in 1936, and comprised ten open-top double-deck bogie trams from Bournemouth, together with a four-wheel works-car-cum-rail-grinder from Poole tramways, which, in turn, replaced an earlier works car from the former Leamington & Warwick Tramways. Mr Hamilton visited Bournemouth to make his selection on site and it is understood that in making his choice particular attention was paid to the amount of tread left on the wheel tyres. The trams were repainted externally in Bournemouth (a task that would have taken forever in Llandudno given their pace of working!). Their green livery has caused modellers of Llandudno trams endless arguments, but the colour most popularly remembered is the green in which they arrived in late 1936/early 1937, which was based on a mix of Cadmium Yellow with a touch of Ultramarine. In later years various shades of green would appear, and this is where opinions differed. The explanation was simple enough: when a tram required a repaint the shade of green was whatever happened to be in the local paint suppliers' shops at the time!

Although objections to the operation of double-deck trams had again been lodged by the respective Councils to the Board of Trade, sanction for their use over the whole line was given with the proviso that should the wind speed on the exposed private road along Penrhyn Bay exceed 50 mph, passengers must be brought down from the upper deck. An anemometer was installed by the toll gate for this purpose, but it eventually fell into disuse.

Now that the fleet had been upgraded, the remainder of the 1907 cars not required were scrapped, several components being kept for spares. Four of these trams were retained and re-numbered (see the following Fleet

An incident has delayed the trams on Mostyn Street during the summer of 1953. A coach belonging to the Birmingham & Midland Motor Omnibus Co Ltd, working the 8.30 am Llandudno-Birmingham service, has been in collision with Crosville bus KA155 (EFM 578), which is running empty back to its depot on Mostyn Broadway. The incident has attracted a large crowd and one of the ex-Bournemouth trams can be seen in the background. *Roy Anderson collection, Gwynedd Archives*

Summary). The four-wheel 'Yankee' cars were also withdrawn and stored in the depot yard.

Attention now turned to the ongoing problems of track and road repairs. A lot of patching up work was done to the track, but the company was never in a position to really get to grips with the situation. It was a problem that dragged on throughout the remaining years of the trams. The overhead wire was completely replaced in 1938 and opportunity was taken to use new hangers as far as funds would allow, although many of the original fittings were adapted to accommodate the new grooved wire, which replaced the former round profile.

Benefits from its efforts were just beginning to be felt by the company when, in August 1939, war was declared. It had been widely expected, and thousands of families had taken holidays not knowing when it would be possible to do so again. The tramway might have suffered drastic financial consequences but for the relocation of various Government offices to both Llandudno and Colwyn Bay together with the transfer of their staff. The result was to be nearly six years of healthy income for the company; its winter takings saw so dramatic an increase that in 1946 Sir Joseph Nall was able to announce a healthy financial position.

On 8 November 1945 car 16, one of the remaining 1907 bogie trams, caught fire in the Bodafon fields and was so badly damaged that it had to be scrapped. The same winter saw storm damage to the sea wall on Penrhyn Bay with the result that temporary single-line operation was instituted between Little Orme Cafe and the tram depot. The low limestone wall had been breached and water and debris had been cast on to the Marine Drive toll road. It was repaired, but a weak spot had been exposed that would cause real problems in future years.

In the spring of 1946 it came to the company's attention that the Darwen tramway system was closing, and that the two totally enclosed streamlined double-deck trams operating there were available. Both trams were thought suitable for winter service on the North Wales

line, and the L&CBER snapped them up for a mere £400 each, together with what few spare parts existed. They were dispatched by road in August 1946 and were put on timber trestles inside the depot. Their bogies were re-gauged by Messrs E. E. Baguley Ltd, Engineers, at Burton-upon-Trent, and eventually re-united with their bodies at Rhos-on-Sea. Repainted and renumbered, the cars looked magnificent as they awaited inspection by the Ministry of Transport, which took place on 14 April 1948.

Unfortunately the Inspector was not happy about the possible effects that the wind would have on totally enclosed streamlined bodies when traversing the open stretches of line on Penrhyn Bay and during the climb up Penrhyn Hill. Neither was he happy about the brake system employed on the trucks, and consequently restricted their use to local services at each end of the line. He stipulated that no passengers should be carried on board when the trams traversed Penrhyn Hill. These questionable decisions were a major disappointment to the company, which either did not know how to overcome the problem or did not want to spend money on the solution. Magnetic brakes could have been fitted to each bogie, but it is quite possible that these parts were difficult to obtain just after the war. One would have thought that, with other tramways closing down, suitable equipment might have been found.

At the time that Baguley did the re-gauging, piping for the compressed air system was replaced. Steam piping was unobtainable, and gas piping, which was considerably weaker, was used as a substitute; it worked, but led to serious problems later on. Had more thought gone into the matter at the time, there is little doubt whatsoever that these two trams could have been the best purchase the company ever made. Warm and comfortable, they would have won back quite a lot of the regular winter traffic that had begun to drift away.

Limited as they were in their operation, they projected a modern image quite unlike anything used on the line before, and although the rule was to drive them 'in

Ex-Darwen streamlined tram No 23, at Penrhyn Bay minus a trolley rope, on driver-training duties prior to the inspection by the Ministry of Transport in 1948. Only six drivers were passed out to drive these trams; Herbert Pitman assessed and trained them and worked No 23 himself on its first day in service. *A. Cocking FRPS*

In service at last! Ex-Darwen tram No 23 is seen at Palladium Corner in June 1948 about to depart for West Shore, as tram No 13 turns into Mostyn Street. Its appearance has attracted the eye of two ladies on the pavement. *Photographer unknown*

series', making them a bit slower than the ex-Bournemouth cars, they gave an infinitely more comfortable ride. Some staff did 'open them up', and then their true acceleration, speed and power showed. Little wonder that the staff nicknamed them the 'Spivs' (a misused expression of the day to denote something posh).

Storms during the winter of 1947 battered the coasts of the United Kingdom and the sea defences were badly damaged along the North Wales coast. The West Shore area of Llandudno was badly affected with flooding to local properties. The wall was breached again at Penrhyn Bay, this time the sea forcing large concrete blocks across the tram tracks together with tons of loose shingle from the beach. The water undermined the tracks and flooded parts of the Rhos-on-Sea Golf Club. The tram service was operated to both sides of the blockage, passengers walking between the obstructions to change trams, not pleasant in high wind and soaked by sea spray.

Shortly after this occurrence the company installed crossover points near Maesgwyn Road and the Golf House to facilitate single-line operation should it be necessary in the future. Following these incidents, both Llandudno and Colwyn Bay Councils drew up plans for sea defences in their respective areas. During 1949 a scheme for Penrhyn Bay estimated at £150,000 was put forward to all frontagers, including the tramway company, for approval and also to find out what contributions

towards the cost could be made. These would be balanced against a grant from Central Government for Sea Defence Works. The matter was to drag on for a further six years before any construction was commenced.

In the meantime the tramway was enjoying something of a revival. The last of the civil servants who had been based in the area had returned to London and people were thronging to the coastal resorts around the country for their annual summer holidays. Signs that things were beginning to change, however, could be seen by the increase in ownership of private motor cars. As the austere years of war fell away, people gradually found that they had more money for luxuries, and for many a car was a priority. Traffic receipts on the tramway were looking reasonable, but the heavy costs of maintenance and labour meant that things which should have been attended to were being deferred. The track and roadway in Llandudno was getting into a dreadful condition, and the Llandudno UDC referred the company to the Ministry of Transport over its lack of track and road repairs. The track was so bad in the town that by 1952 the two streamlined trams could no longer operate there due to damage being caused to their air brake systems, and they were confined to the Colwyn Bay local service. Eventually the company were forced into a programme of repairs on Mostyn Street and Mostyn Broadway, the latter having a particularly bad foundation.

An event that caused major upheaval for every household and business in the area was the conversion by the Merseyside & North Wales Electricity Board of their electricity supply from DC to AC. This conversion would eventually affect the tramway, but when introduced on 15

February 1951 it did not cause any problems because the DC supply for traction current and other assorted outlets was retained by both Llandudno and Colwyn Bay power stations.

Mother nature reared her head again in early January 1952 when ferocious gales producing 20-feet-high waves relentlessly battered the North Wales coast. The new 961-yards-long sea defences at West Shore held firm and protected people and property in the near vicinity from the sea, but Penrhyn Bay and the tram track suffered badly. Waves ate into the rise upon which the tramway ran, flushing away much of the subsoil and ballast from beneath the seaward track and exposing parts of the sleepers. In an attempt to protect what had now become the weakest and most vulnerable part of the line, a member of the tramway staff suggested using a tram to winch boulders from the beach up to the main problem area. By doing this and then back-filling with ballast, it was hoped to at least afford some protection to the tramway.

Tram 17, one of the two surviving 1907 cars, was used. First a large pulley wheel nearly 2 feet in diameter was fixed to the track Next a long wire rope was attached to the bumper of No 17, fed around the pulley wheel and drawn out on to the beach where it was slung around a large boulder. As the tram was driven slowly in reverse it pulled the boulder up the beach to the exact spot where it was required. The rope was then released and staff pulled it back to the beach as the tram moved forward again. Another boulder was selected and the process was repeated, over and over again until the weakened area had been sufficiently reinforced. It was a laborious job that took some weeks to complete, but sadly this sterling effort was dashed to bits the following winter when a larger stretch of track had its foundations washed away. Single-line operation then became a permanent feature, wire fencing being erected between the rails of the seaward tram track to prevent people slipping over the edge.

As a further consequence of this damage, almost all the remaining original lattice poles that had been supporting the overhead wires from bracket arms in the vicinity of Penrhyn Bay were replaced by tubular poles purchased from Sunderland Corporation. The few poles on the seaward side of the line supporting span wires became redundant and were eventually removed.

Naturally the event attracted press attention and many people went to have a look. Among the interested personages was W. J. Crosland-Taylor, the General Manager of Crosville Motor Services Ltd. It looked not only to him but also to the casual observer that the days of the trams were numbered. Crosville was keen to get its hands on the tramway and shut it down. Crosland-Taylor set a task for his Management Trainees' examination in March 1953. He asked them to assume that the tramway was cut in two by the sea and closed. Students were to study the area and make recommendations as to how the area would be most economically served by Crosville. This was an interesting and forward-thinking move, but the tram company was not defeated yet!

On 17 September 1952 Mr Hamilton died; he was 78 and had been General Manager for 21 years. His position was not filled immediately, Assistant Manager Mr H. T. Jones assuming responsibility for the day-to-day affairs. Walter Butterworth, who had been brought in from Manchester earlier in the year as Works Superintendent, was responsible for the maintenance side of the job. One wonders if his experience with buses was the factor that led Sir Joseph Nall to offer him the position at Llandudno. There can be little doubt that the L&CBER Board of Directors were giving serious consideration to the operation of buses, and it really became a matter of timing. Whenever the end came, the company was going to be liable for a hefty road-reinstatement bill following the lifting of the tram tracks, so it was a question of keeping the trams going until a point of no return in their decline was reached.

The two streamlined trams continued to work the Colwyn Bay local service during 1953 until No 23 broke a bearing, and spares that had been lying in the shed suddenly 'could not be found', rendering the tram inoperative. Its air compressor was removed and installed in the blacksmith's area at the depot. The following year No 24 was in the depot having its air compressor dismantled to cure some '. . . real or imagined fault. Some key components went missing or were lost, ensuring that the compressor would not operate again and therefore, no air, no tram'. Neither 23 nor 24 would ever run again. If the wind of change was in the air, did it have a helping hand or was it simply down to gross incompetence?

During 1954 Mostyn Broadway received attention. Parts of the track were repacked and the road surface made good. To maintain the service without disruption, a pair of points were installed near Tudor Road to minimise the distance that trams would have to operate 'wrong line' around the excavated tracks. This crossover also enabled trams to reverse quickly when dealing with the queues of people leaving the Arcadia and Grand theatres. As the work progressed, trams operated 'wrong line' between Tudor Road and the library in Mostyn Street.

In November 1954, at their Annual General Meeting, the Directors announced that in September they had applied to the North Western Traffic Commissioners for a Road Service Licence to operate buses. In October the Chairman of the Commissioners had insisted that a timetable would have to be drawn up and agreed with Crosville before any bus services could be operated by the L&CBER. Llandudno and Colwyn Bay Councils objected to the abandonment of the tramway on the grounds that the responsibility of road reinstatement had not been clarified. Following a joint meeting between the local Councils, the company and the Ministry of Transport, no decision was reached. The Councils were convinced that the road problem lay with the tram company.

Another body-blow was dealt by MANWEB, which advised the L&CBER that from June 1956 it would require £100 per day to staff the two power stations supplying the traction current. If this was not possible, MANWEB suggested that the company take the generating plant and install it behind or adjacent to the tram depot. Financial constraints precluded the company from taking up either of the suggestions. The company mortgaged its depot, two semi-detached houses and a small quarry on the Little Orme in 1954, most probably to enable them to fund the conversion programme. Later still it obtained an overdraft against the sale of the overhead copper wire

LLANDUDNO & COLWYN BAY ELECTRIC RAILWAY,
LIMITED.

CHAIRMAN'S STATEMENT

For the convenience of shareholders, I am circulating a statement this year, instead of making these remarks at the Annual General Meeting as in previous years.

Despite all our efforts the results of the year under review have been the worst for many years. The costs of nearly all materials have risen and there has been a further increase in wages, but it is to the costs of Repairs and Maintenance and Motive Power that the main increases can be attributed. In the case of Motive Power the agreements for the supply of electricity were terminated by the Supply Authority during 1953. So far no new agreements have been settled and in the Accounts we have had to estimate the costs for the year. To meet the increased expenses the Company successfully applied to the Ministry of Transport to increase the statutory maximum fare from 1d. to 2d. a mile, and in July 1953 a revised scale of fares was introduced. As a result of this increase in fares the Revenue for the year was £30,906 compared with £31,137 in the previous year although the number of passengers carried fell from 2,744,693 to 2,607,994.

The Directors have for some time been considering the advisibility of substituting motor omnibuses in place of the trams, and as a first step towards this, application is being made to the Licensing Authority for the grant of a Road Service Licence. It is considered that the operation of motor omnibuses, although not possessing the present day novelty of trams, would be more attractive to the travelling public and of benefit to the Company.

JOSEPH NALL,
Chairman.

Llandudno & Colwyn Bay Electric Railway,
Limited

Directors :

COLONEL SIR JOSEPH NALL, Bart., D.S.O., Chairman.
STANLEY DUDMAN, M.Inst.T.   JOHN R. AMPHLETT, LL.B.

Secretary and Registered Office :
D. R. P. BAKER,
SUFFOLK HOUSE, LAURENCE POUNTNEY HILL, LONDON, E.C.4.

REPORT OF THE DIRECTORS

To be submitted to the Members at the FORTY-EIGHTH ANNUAL GENERAL MEETING *to be held at* SUFFOLK HOUSE, LAURENCE POUNTNEY HILL *in the* CITY OF LONDON, *on* WEDNESDAY, *the* 10TH *day of* NOVEMBER, 1954, *at* NOON.

The Directors present the audited accounts of the Company as at 31st December, 1953. The comparative figures for 1952 are also furnished.

There was a decrease of £250 in receipts and an increase of £1,532 in expenses.

The loss of £3,004 on Profit and Loss Account compares with a loss of £1,222 last year. All repairs and renewals have been charged to revenue and no provision has been made for depreciation of fixed assets.

In view of the carrying forward of losses (as computed for Income Tax) in previous years, it is considered unnecessary to make any provision for taxation in the present accounts.

Sir Joseph Nall retires from the Board by rotation and offers himself for re-election.

Messrs. Hays, Akers & Hays have signified their willingness to continue in office as auditors, and a Resolution will be proposed relative to their remuneration.

By Order of the Board,

D. R. P. BAKER,
Secretary.

SUFFOLK HOUSE,
LAURENCE POUNTNEY HILL,
LONDON, E.C.4.

18th October, 1954.

Report to the Directors and Chairman's Statement regarding the proposal to change over to motor buses, October 1954. Note that receipts are down by £250 but expenses up by £1,532. By comparison with today these figures seem very small, but in 1954 they were becoming unacceptable. *Author's collection*

and brass fittings that enabled them to purchase second-hand buses to replace the trams.

During 1955 there were good traffic returns, holiday-makers enjoying a long and warm summer. That year also saw a start on the new sea wall incorporating a promenade along the Marine Drive and toll road; it was eventually completed in the early part of 1956. Meanwhile news of the trams' imminent demise spread among tram enthusiasts.

A preservation committee was quickly formed and a nationwide appeal went out to raise sufficient funds to buy the unique tramway. Its efforts had the support of a prominent L&CBER Director, and as monies flowed in items of essential equipment were bought and stored in readiness for transporting to North Wales. The line had been surveyed so the committee were well aware of what needed to be done. Among vital items gathered together were three sets of automatic electrical control equipment, which would enable the power to be supplied, unmanned, to the tramway. It is understood that MAN-WEB was sympathetic to the situation and offered facilities to have the plant installed on its premises. The third set of control equipment was to have been installed at the foot of Penrhyn Hill as a back-up if required.

By the end of 1955 a sum of money matching that which the tram company required initially (an unconfirmed £7,500) had been raised. Early in January 1956, although no date for the conversion had been announced, the work of scrapping the trams began. Trams 1, 2, 9 and 10 were broken up by members of the tramway staff. Further talks about preservation suddenly floundered, and here the story becomes rather vague, due to the passing of time and the inevitable loss of those people who were involved. Having raised the money initially required, the preservation group were faced with a further two increases in the asking price by the Board, who appeared to have had a change of heart, thinking that they would make greater financial gains by operating buses. In view of the massive expenditure that would have been involved immediately after the take-over, not the least of which would have been track renewal and road reinstatement, the preservationists began to get cold feet and decided, rightly so, that they were not prepared to pay a grossly inflated asking price (an unconfirmed sum of £30,000) for an operation that needed a lot of money to be poured into essential works from the outset. The system's book value would have probably had difficulty reaching a figure of even £18,000, including all the freehold assets. It became obvious, too, that the Board did not want to see someone else make a success of the tramway. Comparisons between this attempted take-over and the successful bid by railway enthusiasts, so ably led by the late L. T. C. Rolt, which secured the Talyllyn Railway in 1951 would be a little unfair, as the operating conditions of the two enterprises were so very different.

All monies raised were returned to the subscribers with a letter, part of which stated that due to the fact that four tramcars had been scrapped, the project was no longer considered viable. No precise reason was ever given as to the failure. I now believe it could be best summarised as a battle of wills, a lack of working capital over and above any purchase monies raised, and cold feet. The outcome

was a bitter disappointment to those closely involved, and the eventual loss of this unique tramway was felt by a great many people throughout the United Kingdom who knew the line.

Bus driver training was already under way and the vehicle used was an ex-East Kent Leyland Titan dating from 1938, which had arrived at Rhos-on-Sea depot in September 1955. Training was carried out under the tuition of Evan Jones, and the first two men to pass the Public Service Vehicle test were Alf Harris and John Glyn Jones. Eventually more buses arrived and went into the depot for overhaul and repaint.

Modifications had to be carried out to the depot, which was still full of trams, including the filling in of the pits and the provision of a fuel tank. The trams were shunted on to the left-hand side of the depot, occupying roads 4 to 8 inclusive, with some parked right at the back of roads 1 and 2.

The date of the last tram was announced as 24 March 1956, and on that day hundreds of tram enthusiasts took their last rides. For the local travelling public it was a normal Saturday, the most noticeable difference being that it was more difficult to get a seat on the tram and there were a lot of people carrying cameras. The four trams in service on the last day were ex-Accrington 3 and 4, and ex-Bournemouth 11 and 14. No 11 broke her lifeguard negotiating the points at Maesgwyn Road in mid-afternoon and was replaced by No 13.

Tram No 8 was reserved for a party of former Bournemouth tram drivers who had travelled from the South Coast through the night in a Bournemouth bus, provided free for them by Bournemouth Corporation Transport. They took turns driving the tram over the entire route under the watchful eye of Chief Inspector Ernie Woolley. Being out of practice, one motorman fluffed his attempt to climb Penrhyn Hill and the tram reversed almost to St David's corner for another run to be made, this time with success! Treated to a buffet lunch by the company, the party returned to Bournemouth later in the afternoon, while No 8 was cleaned and made ready for the ceremonial last journey later in the evening.

Farmer Dick Hughes, the longest-serving employee, had been driving No 14 on early shift, and when he finished he went home to Old Colwyn and brought his granddaughter back for a last look at the trams. He returned home with her, had a meal, 'got spruced up' and made his way back to the depot where he teamed up with Bob Morgan, the longest-serving conductor. Together they took the tram through to Llandudno to meet the official party, who were enjoying cocktails at the Imperial Hotel. Although they had instructions not to carry passengers, two enthusiasts were picked up at Orme Point and were both amazed when Dick let one of them 'have a turn on the handles' through Bodafon Fields. The two lads jumped off just before the tram arrived at the North Western Hotel.

At 10.20 pm the civic party and other distinguished guests boarded the tram and, under the guidance of Farmer Dick, Councillor John Owen, Chairman of the Llandudno Urban District, took the controls and drove No 8 to West Shore. The last public service tram, No 4, had already passed on its last through journey to Colwyn Bay.

No 8 left West Shore nearly 20 minutes late due to a controller problem that had delayed the previous tram's departure, and made its way through the streets of Llandudno accompanied by motorists and witnessed by groups of people gathered at street corners to see her go by. After a brief pause at Nant-y-Gamar Road, the tram entered the darkness of Bodafon Fields and began the long climb up past Craigside to the top of Penrhyn Hill, where a large crowd from the village of Penrhynside had gathered. Amid cheering and singing, Ernie Woolley took the controls for the descent of Penrhyn Hill. On reaching Rhos Depot, there was another delay while No 4 was replaced by No 3, the former having developed a fault that all but totally incapacitated her.

Now driven by the Mayor of Colwyn Bay, Councillor Edward Hughes, No 8 followed No 3 at a discreet distance. Their arrival and departure from Colwyn Bay was witnessed by another large crowd, both trams eventually arriving back at the depot after midnight. The large crowd there cheered and waved as No 8, driven by Chief Inspector Ernie Woolley, left the roadway for a place in local transport history. The last privately owned street tramway in the British Isles had finally died.

Joe Bellamy, who lived next door to the depot, brought his accordion out and started to play 'Auld Lang Syne', accompanied by the entire throng gathered there. Guests were taken back to Llandudno in one of the replacement buses driven by Alf Harris, which was loudly booed out of the depot yard. Later that morning, the first two 'Red' buses (as they were to become known) took to the road,

crewed by Alf Harris with conductor Bob Morgan, and John Glyn Jones with conductress Rene Johnson. It was the beginning of the last phase in the company's history. Buses were never going to provide the answer to the financial fortunes of the company, particularly second-hand utility-bodied vehicles operating in direct competition with the latest buses that Crosville could and did throw into the fray.

The bus route, in the main, followed the tram route but diverted away from the unmade sections of private roads and reserved tracks. In Colwyn Bay the terminus was located near the railway station in Seaview Road.

The trams were scrapped during the spring and summer of 1956. By October, with the exception of ex-Bournemouth No 6, which had been bought by a Mr Richardson of Rhyl for preservation, only the two 'Spivs' remained. They were a different proposition from the wooden-bodied cars that had already been dispatched, and the contractors tried to find a buyer for them to save themselves the expensive job of cutting them up. As no buyers were found, the pair were eventually cut up on site.

The saga of the lifting of the track came to the fore. In the April immediately following abandonment of the tramway, rails were lifted from all reserved trackbeds, along Glan-y-Mor Road as far as the junction with Morfa Road, then the seaward track between the Golf House and Orme Point. The local authorities were adamant that the terms relating to the tram track specified that if the tramway was abandoned the rails must be lifted and the

Llandudno No 6 has been restored to Bournemouth Corporation Tramways livery and has assumed her original fleet number 85. The restoration was carried out at the Bournemouth bus under- taking's Mallard Road workshops in 1974, and the tram is pictured attending a local transport rally some time later. *'2489' Group, courtesy of S. E. Letts*

road replaced in the condition to which it was before the tramway was built. Interestingly, there were few roads in existence when the tramway was built, so the company simply removed the rails laid in Penrhyn Avenue between Orme Point and Colwyn Crescent, filling in the area with compressed hard-core, and claiming that the road was then better than it had been in 1907! This effectively left Penrhyn Avenue with a strip of asphalt about 8 feet wide the full length of the road on the seaward side, the rest being gravel. The track that passed along Gloddaeth Avenue in Llandudno adjacent to the central grass strip was dealt with in similar fashion. The two local authorities were understandably beside themselves with anger. They mustered the support of the two County Councils, Caernarvonshire and Denbighshire, to take combined action against the company.

Although Penrhyn Avenue (then still a private road) was fully reconstructed by Colwyn Bay Council with the aid of an £18,000 loan in October 1957 ('Red' buses operating towards Llandudno traversed the parallel Abbey Road), the arguments went on for two years. They culminated in a joint meeting of Highway Authorities, including the Divisional Road Engineer, following the decision by the Ministry of Transport that the company be divested of its powers over the highways, under Section 71 of the Light Railway Order of 1898, unless before 31 January 1958 agreement had been reached over the tram track.

As no agreement was reached, the company was directed to pay the sum of £5,000 to the Highway Authorities, that sum being accepted in settlement of the company's liability for maintenance of track. The Highway Authorities indemnified the company against all claims for accidents or injuries from the date of payment, but stipulated that the company abandon all claims to rails and any equipment not removed except any traction poles that the Council (Colwyn Bay) may wish to purchase. The Order divesting the company of its powers was confirmed by the Ministry of Transport and Civil Aviation under The Llandudno & Colwyn Bay Light Railway (Cessor of Powers) Order 1958, dated 25 April of that year.

From that stage onward, the principal problems were concerned with revenue. The competition was fierce and, despite published timetables with agreed duplication, the battle with Crosville seemed never-ending, particularly during the summer months when every passenger mattered. Notices appeared in the Rhos-on-Sea depot warning drivers not to race against the opposition, but it still persisted. Both companies were in and out of the Traffic Commissioner's courts objecting to what the other side was doing. Some points debated were so trivial that they were merely a waste of money spent on legal fees. It couldn't continue, and it didn't.

In late April 1961 Crosville made a £40,000 bid for the 'goodwill' of the tram company, and the Directors recommended to the shareholders that it be accepted. The take-over became effective from 28 May, the last 'Red' bus running into Rhos-on-Sea depot on Saturday 27th. It was driven by M. K. Morris and conducted by his brother-in-law, John Peacock. The event passed without ceremony. A few of the staff left prior to closure, most of the others being employed by Crosville, which had also taken the opportunity to modify its services throughout the district.

There remained the problems of the toll road, together with various other properties that the company still owned. A Special Resolution was passed on 14 November 1961 that the company be wound up voluntarily, the Liquidators continuing to collect tolls until, in 1963, both the toll road and depot were sold. Glan-y-Mor Road and the former Marine Drive toll road were formally adopted by the respective highway authorities and properly made up during 1964. Later that year the two semi-detached houses were sold and the sale of the parcel of land on Penrhyn Hill followed in 1965. The Company was formally wound up on 16 December 1966, its total assets realising £57,227 10s 0d.

THE LLANDUDNO & COLWYN BAY ELECTRIC RAILWAY LTD.
JOURNEY WAY BILL

CONDUCTOR'S NAME ....

MOTORMAN'S NAME ....

CAR No. .... DATE ....

18050—Williamson, Ticket Printer, Ashton.

OPENING NUMBER OF TICKETS AND NUMBER OF TICKETS ISSUED

TRIP No.	TIME LEAVING Hrs. Mins.	STAGE	1d OPENING No.	No. ISSUED	1½d OPENING No.	No. ISSUED	2d OPENING No.	No. ISSUED	3d OPENING No.	No. ISSUED	4d OPENING No.	No. ISSUED	5d OPENING No.	No. ISSUED	6d OPENING No.	No. ISSUED	7d OPENING No.	No. ISSUED	8d OPENING No.	No. ISSUED	9d OPENING No.	No. ISSUED	1/- RETURN OPENING No.	No. ISSUED	EXCHANGES BLUE OPENING No.	No. ISSUED	OPENING No.	No. ISSUED	PUNCH REGISTER	INSPEC-TOR'S INITIALS	WEEKLY TICKETS Workmen's	No. ISSUED
1		COLWYN BAY																													6d	
		KING'S RD.																													9d	
		RHOS RD.																													1/-	
		CHURCH RD.																													1/6	
		QUARRY COT.																													2/-	
		PENRHYN HILL																													2/6	
		BRYN-Y-BIA																													3/-	
		NANT-Y-GAMAR																													3/6	
		CARMEN S. RD.																														
		ST. JOHN'S																													Scholars' 5 DAYS 6d	
2		WEST SHORE																													9d	
		HOOSON'S C'RNER																													10d	
		ST. JOHN'S																													1/-	
		QUEEN'S RD.																													1/3	
		NANT-Y-GAMAR																													1/8	
		PENRHYN HILL																													1/10½	
		L. ORME CAFE																													2/3	
		QUARRY COT.																														
		ORME POINT																														
		RHOS RD.																														
		EBBERSTON RD.																														
3		COLWYN BAY																														
		KING'S RD.																														
		RHOS RD.																														
		CHURCH RD.																														
		QUARRY COT.																														
		PENRHYN HILL																														
		BRYN-Y-BIA																														
		NANT-Y-GAMAR																														
		CARMEN S. RD.																														
		ST. JOHN'S																														
4		WEST SHORE																														
		HOOSON'S C'RNER																														
		ST. JOHN'S																														
		QUEEN'S RD.																														
		NANT-Y-GAMAR																														
		PENRHYN HILL																														
		L. ORME CAFE																														
		QUARRY COT.																														
		ORME POINT																														
		RHOS RD.																														
		EBBERSTON RD.																														

Above 'Journey way bill' for recording the quantity of tickets of different values sold. *Author's collection*

Right Costs of Workmen's and Scholars' Weekly Tickets, January 1952. *Author's collection*

Opposite page A selection of L&CBER tickets, reproduced at approximately 90% full size. *Author's collection*

LLANDUDNO & COLWYN BAY ELECTRIC RAILWAY LTD.

Workmen's Weekly Tickets
AND
Scholars' 5-days' Weekly Tickets

The above are issued by Conductors and can also be purchased at the Car Depot, Rhos-on-Sea, in accordance with the Scale of Charges set out below.

Where the Ordinary Single Fares are	Workmen's Weekly are	Scholars' Weekly 5 days only
	s. d.	s. d.
1½d.	9	9
2d.	1 0	10
3d.	1 6	1 0
4d.	2 0	1 3
5d.	2 6	1 8
6d.	3 0	1 10½
7d.	3 6	2 3

Workmen's Weekly Tickets are issued on Mondays and are available for six days, during the week of issue only, for one outward journey and one return journey each day, subject to the first journey each day being completed before 9 a.m.

Scholars' Weekly Tickets are issued on Monday and Tuesday mornings and are available, during the week of issue only, for two outward journeys and two return journeys each day—from Monday to Friday inclusive.

These Scholars' Tickets are available to bona-fide school children, up to their Sixteenth birthday, during term time and then only for travelling to and from school.

Tramway Depot, Rhos-on-Sea.

JAN., 1952.

W. G. HAMILTON, A.M.I.E.E. General Manager.

POWLSONS, THE COLWYN BAY PRESS

MP 6603
LLANDUDNO & COLWYN
BAY ELECTRIC RLY. LTD.

STAGE	1d	STAGE
1		12
2		11
3		10
4		9
5		8
6		7
7		6
8		5
9		4
11		2
12		1

Ticket is to be punched in the section to which Passenger is entitled to travel, and must be shown on demand. Issued subject to the Bye-laws.
AUTO-TICKETS LTD. BIRKENHEAD

CB 9128
LLANDUDNO & COLWYN
BAY ELECTRIC RLY. LTD.

	1½d	
1		12
2		11
3		10
4		9
5		8
7		6
9		4
10		3
11		2
12		1

AUTO-TICKETS LTD. BIRKENHEAD

FH 3701
LLANDUDNO & COLWYN
BAY ELECTRIC RLY. LTD.

STAGE	2d	STAGE
1		8
2		7
3		6
4		5
5		4
6		3
7		2
8		1
DOG		DOG

AUTO-TICKETS LIMITED. BIRKENHEAD

RV 1708
LLANDUDNO & COLWYN
BAY ELECTRIC RLY. LTD.

Stage	3d	Stage
1		8
2		7
3		6
4		5
5		4
6		3
7		2
8		1

Ticket is to be punched in the section to which Passenger is entitled to travel, and must be shown on demand within it to the Bye-laws.
AUTO-TICKETS LTD. BIRKENHEAD

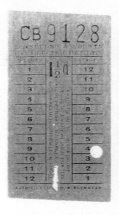

AB 4065
LLANDUDNO & COLWYN
BAY ELECTRIC RLY. LTD.

Stage	4d	Stage
1		8
2		7
3		6
4		5
5		4
6		3
7		2
8		1

Ticket is to be punched in the section to which Passenger is entitled to travel, and must be shown on demand. Issued subject to the Bye-laws.
AUTO-TICKETS LTD. BIRKENHEAD

HH 5136
LLANDUDNO & COLWYN
BAY ELECTRIC RLY. LTD.

Stage	5d	Stage
1		6
2		5
3		4
4		3
5		2
6		1

Ticket is to be punched in the section to which Passenger is entitled to travel, and must be shown on demand. Issued subject to the Bye-laws.
AUTO-TICKETS LTD. BIRKENHEAD

IE 0085
LLANDUDNO & COLWYN
BAY ELECTRIC RLY. LTD.

Stage	6d	Stage
1		6
2		5
3		4
4		3
5		2
6		1

Ticket is to be punched in the section to which Passenger is entitled to travel, and must be shown on demand. Issued subject to the Bye-laws.
AUTO-TICKETS LTD. BIRKENHEAD

SA 3091
LLANDUDNO & COLWYN
BAY ELECTRIC RLY. LTD.

Stage	7d	Stage
1		6
2		5
3		4
4		3
5		2
6		1

Ticket is to be punched in the section to which Passenger is entitled to travel, and must be shown on demand. Issued subject to the Bye-laws.

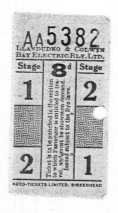

AA 5382
LLANDUDNO & COLWYN
BAY ELECTRIC RLY. LTD.

Stage	8d	Stage
1		2
2		1

Ticket is to be punched in the section to which Passenger is entitled to travel, and must be shown on demand. Issued subject to the Bye-laws.
AUTO-TICKETS LIMITED. BIRKENHEAD

C 1471
LLANDUDNO & COLWYN
BAY ELECTRIC RLY. LTD.

Stage	9d	
1		
		Stage
		1

Ticket is to be punched in the section to which Passenger is entitled to travel, and must be shown on demand. Issued subject to the Bye-laws.
AUTO-TICKETS LIMITED. BIRKENHEAD

SI 2735
LLANDUDNO & COLWYN
BAY ELECTRIC RLY. LTD.

EXCHANGE TICKET
NOT TO BE CHARGED FOR

OUT		
2d		2d
3d		3d
4d		4d
5d		5d
6d		6d
7d		7d
8d		8d
9d		9d

Only given in exchange for a Ticket previously issued by this Company. Value of ticket surrendered. Available for journey on which issued only. Must be shown for inspection and given up on demand. Subject to Bye-laws and Regulations.

March 24th 1956
LLANDUDNO & COLWYN
BAY ELECTRIC RLY. LTD.

Stage		Stage
	SOUVENIR	
2	LAST	5
3	TRAM	4
4	JOURNEY	3
6		1

AUTO-TICKETS LTD. BIRKENHEAD

BD 5777
LLANDUDNO & COLWYN BAY
ELECTRIC RAILWAY LTD.

2D RETURN

This Ticket must be produced whole on the return journey.

STAGE	2d. RETURN	STAGE
1		8
2		9
3		
		11
		12
		13
7		14

Must be shown for inspection & given up on demand. Issued subject to Bye-laws and Regulations.
BD 5777

ML 5870
LLANDUDNO & COLWYN
BAY ELECTRIC RLY. LTD.

Stage		Stage
1		6
2	2D	5
3		4
4		3
5		2
6		1

AUTO-TICKETS LTD. BIRKENHEAD

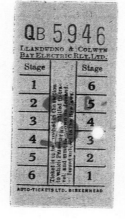

QB 5946
LLANDUDNO & COLWYN
BAY ELECTRIC RLY. LTD.

Stage		Stage
1		6
2		5
3		4
4		3
5		2
6		1

Ticket is to be punched in the section to which Passenger is entitled to travel, and must be shown on demand. Issued subject to the Bye-laws.
AUTO-TICKETS LTD. BIRKENHEAD

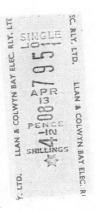

LLAN. & COLWYN BAY ELEC. RLY. LTD.

SINGLE

APR 13
A 0087951

PENCE
4
SHILLINGS

LLAN & COLWYN BAY ELEC. RLY. LTD.

When talking to people not interested in the trams, but who did ride on them in Llandudno, the one feature that stands out in their memories was the ride through Bodafon Fields. Brought vividly back to life in this view, heavily laden ex-Bournemouth tram No 7 begins the long climb past Craigside towards Penrhyn Hill in August 1955. Crops in the fields towards the Promenade are about ready for harvesting, having ripened during the warm summer. *Colour-Rail (IR 258)*

A particularly busy scene in Mostyn Street outside Marks & Spencer. 'Toast-rack' No 21 is taking passengers on board and the driver checks to see that everyone is clear of the tram before moving off. The signal to start would be given by the conductor with two loud blasts on his 'Acme Thunderer' whistle. The same system was used when conductors were collecting fares on the open-top double-deck trams. A pre-war Ford 8 car passes on the left. *Colour Rail (IR 167)*

Ex-Accrington single-deck tram No 4 descends Penrhyn Hill. This was one of the parts of the route that gave the line its 'interurban' look and feel. Two motor cars can be seen on the main Llandudno Road. *Jim Copland*

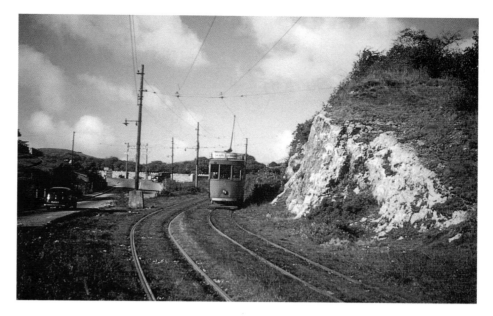

Photographed leaving the promenade at Rhos-on-Sea, one of the original surviving 1907 trams, No 17, negotiates the reverse curves leading along the short Caley Promenade on its journey to Colwyn Bay. On this spring day in 1955, the sea looks relatively calm. *Leeds Transport Historical Society*

The end of the line! By August 1956 only four trams, ex-Darwen streamlined Nos 23 and 24 and open-top double-deckers 11 and 12, remained to be broken up; the streamliner in this view is 24. One of the replacement 'Red' buses can also be seen. *Colour Rail (IR 262)*

FLEET SUMMARY

Prior to opening

Two four-wheel 26-seat single-deck trams were obtained by the contractors from an abandoned tramway project on Canvey Island. They were built by Brush and returned to that company when the new trams began to arrive at Rhos-on-Sea depot later in 1907.

Nos 1-14: single-deck bogie cars

These were built by the Midland Railway Carriage Co Ltd of Shrewsbury, and were mounted on equal-wheel bogie trucks by Mountain & Gibson Ltd of Bury. They were of special design for light railway work and were fitted with four 30 hp motors per car, giving a total of 120 hp. Hand-wheel brakes were fitted in addition to the Westinghouse magnetic brakes.

The bodies had vestibule ends, monitor roofs and end platforms with an entrance on each side. The saloons comprised two compartments, one for smoking, the other for non-smoking passengers; there was longitudinal seating for 42 passengers with 14 standing. The eight windows on each

Original 1907 tram No 14 (pictured on 19 October 1907).

side were arranged to drop down, providing excellent ventilation in the summer months. On delivery some trams were fitted with a single trolley pole mounted centrally, some with two. Eventually all these trams carried two trolleys, which were later stowed under large hooks fitted on the cab roof. No 3 was used for testing purposes during September 1907.

The livery was Midland red and cream ornately lined out in gold, but for the duration of the First World War they were temporarily painted all over in battleship grey.

During 1924-25 the four 30 hp motors were replaced in all of these cars by two BTH GE249 35 hp motors per car, giving a total of 70 hp, a substantial reduction in power with a resultant saving on the use of electrical current. Work on the bodies as required was also undertaken during this period.

The four entrances survived until 1931 when one each side was enclosed, providing the conventional rear entrance-exit facility. By 1937 only four cars of this class remained, the others having been displaced by replacement rolling-stock. The four survivors, Nos 6, 10, 11 and 14, were renumbered 16, 19, 17 and 18 respectively. It was intended that the new No 19 was to be converted to a toast-rack, but that idea was never carried out.

Four-wheel semi-convertible tram No 18 of 1909.

It is possible that the body of this car was cut in half to make a summerhouse for the General Manager's garden! No 16 was scrapped following a fire on board in 1945. No 17 had been intended for use as the official 'Last Tram' in 1956, but was involved in a collision and scrapped before the end. No 18 was effectively withdrawn from service early in 1955 and was stored in the paint shop minus one trolley.

Nos 15-18: four-wheel semi-convertible cars

These trams arrived in September 1909, having been ordered from the United Electric Car Co Ltd of Preston. They looked 'foreign' and were soon nicknamed 'Yankees' by the staff. The bodies were 31 feet long with conventional platforms and eight narrow drop windows to each side. The saloons had transverse seating for 27 people, and the provision of a small bench seat on each platform facing towards the steps brought the seating capacity to 31, with eight standees. Destination boxes were fitted when new but were later removed in favour of destination boards facing forward in the driver's cab window. The livery was a dark red and cream elaborately lined out in gold, the new company name being displayed the full length of the rocker panel.

These cars were originally mounted on 10-foot-wheel-base Warner radial trucks by Mountain & Gibson. Hand-wheel and rheostatic brakes supplemented by magnetic brakes were fitted from new. Undoubtedly the length of the trucks was the root cause of noise on all of the tight

curves along the route of the tramway. Complaints were first made in 1910 and were to continue long after this class had been withdrawn.

In 1927 Brush-built Peckham P35 8 ft 6 in wheelbase trucks with roller-bearings were fitted, together with new electrical equipment. These trams almost took on a life of their own; if driven at speed on level track they were fine, but if at speed there was any undulation in the track, they started to 'pitch and buck about like prairie jack-rabbits'. More than a few passengers complained of sickness during and after riding on them.

All these cars were withdrawn in 1936 and were stored in the depot yard until 1941, when their bodies were sold for sheds to Army camps in Bodelwyddan and Rhyl. The trucks were sold to Leeds City Transport.

Nos 19-22: open 'toast-rack' cars

These trams, so named because they bore a resemblance to the familiar breakfast table utensil, were ordered in 1914 from the United Electric Car Co Ltd but not delivered until 1920. The bodies provided seating for 60 passengers on 14 full-width lift-over bench seats, with two half-width lift-over seats on each side of the trolley mast. They were mounted on a pair of English Electric, Mountain & Gibson-pattern, equal-wheel bogies, each with two BTH GE249 motors. Hand-wheel and magnetic brakes were installed.

These cars were delivered in green and cream with

plain lining surrounding their dash panels. The original lifeguards included a peculiar wire netting 'scoop' protruding in front of the tram, but these were replaced quite early on by V-shaped fixed lifeguards.

In 1937, when one of the original 1907 trams was re-numbered 19, the toast-rack bearing that number became 23, but reverted to its original number when the other tram was scrapped. Nos 19 and 20 received K4 controllers from Sunderland trams in 1954.

Nos 1-5: ex-Accrington single-deck bogie cars

Purchased in 1933, two of these trams, Nos 2 and 5 (Accrington Nos 29 and 32), arrived as complete cars, while the remaining three, Nos 1, 3 and 4 (Accrington 28, 30 and 31) came as bodies only and were mounted on the bogies from the first of the withdrawn 1907 trams. The four Brush Type C maximum-traction bogie trucks that had arrived from Accrington had to be re-gauged from 4 ft 0 in to 3 ft 6 in, and this work was carried out at Rhos-on-Sea depot. Braking was hand-wheel and magnetic. Trams 1, 2 and 5 had car meters fitted to their No 2 end bulkheads in Accrington, and these were left in situ. As built in the 1920-22 period, they had their headlamps mounted on a destination box located on the cab roof, but these were removed and headlamps from the surplus 1907 cars fitted to the dashes.

These trams entered service in their Accrington livery and, with possibly only one exception, carried the Llandudno crest and legal lettering. They had all been re-painted to green and cream by 1936. The original longitu-

dinal wooden bench seats were replaced in 1937-38 with the rattan seating from the withdrawn 1907 cars, enabling 40 passengers to sit in comfort!

During the Second World War the trams were equipped with a small red light fitted behind the windscreen nearest the step as a token warning to motorists during the blackout. Large areas of the bulkhead windows were blacked out and blue bulbs were fitted to the interiors. (The ex-Bournemouth cars were similarly treated.)

No 3 was the last tram to be completely overhauled, refurbished and re-painted. The work was carried out during 1952-53 and, following trials on No 8, moquette seat cushions from Birmingham Tramways were fitted to trams 1-15. The same year all the ex-Accrington trams were fitted with ex-Birmingham self-aligning trolley heads. No 5 was equipped with a pair of GE249 motors from an ex-Bournemouth tram (either 12 or 13) during September.

Nos 6-15: ex-Bournemouth open-top double-deck bogie cars

This group of trams, purchased in 1936, consisted of cars from three batches originally ordered by Bournemouth over the years between 1914 and 1926.

No 6 (Bournemouth 85)

This was the oldest, having been built in 1914 by the United Electric Car Co Ltd. It had a semi-circular dash and was unvestibuled. Accommodating 30 passengers inside and 38 outside, the body was mounted on a pair of Brill 22E maximum-traction bogies, each with Westinghouse

One of the ex-Bournemouth trams, No 12, built in 1924-6. *R. J. S. Wiseman*

226N 40 hp motors. At Llandudno these were eventually exchanged for a pair of GE249 motors from withdrawn 1907 cars 7, 8, 9, 12 or 13 before they were scrapped.

Complete vestibules were fitted in 1921, but this tram was an odd one out. It had a split window nearest the step with curved glass fitted to accommodate the sweep of the driver's handbrake handle. So far as can be judged, this was due to the handbrake column being located slightly closer to the dash than on the other cars - an simple mistake made in the original construction that led to an unusual solution to an awkward problem. At some stage during or immediately after the war, the windscreen was altered at Llandudno, the tram looking basically the same as her sisters.

In November 1953 No 6 was fitted with English Electric DK30B motors with single helical gears and wheelsets from Birmingham. Late in 1955 it was taken out of service with a defective motor. A replacement from No 10 was fitted when that tram was involved in an accident and withdrawn.

No 6 was subsequently purchased by a Mr Richardson of Rhyl for preservation, and after being on display in London for many years, eventually returned to Bournemouth on 15 November 1974, where it was restored to Bournemouth condition.

Nos 9, 10, 11 and 13 (Bournemouth 108, 103, 95 and 112)

These were built in 1921 by Brush and were similar to No 6 except that the bodies were 3 inches wider and they had elliptical rather than semi-circular dashes. The cars were delivered to Bournemouth with vestibules fitted, and their Brill 22E maximum-traction bogies each had two 40 hp BTH GE249A motors fitted.

No 10 was fitted with English Electric DK30B motors and single helical gears from Birmingham in November 1953. It was withdrawn in November 1955, one of its motors going into No 6.

Nos 7, 8, 12, 14 and 15 (Bournemouth 115, 116, 128, 121 and 114)

Built between 1924 and 1926, these cars were similar to the above-mentioned batch. They had Metrovick MV104 40 hp motors, but were re-equipped with BTH GE249A motors at Llandudno. During the period December 1953-February 1954 Nos 8, 12 and 15 were fitted with English Electric DK30B motors (single helical gears on 8 and 15, straight gears on 12) and wheelsets from Birmingham. No 12 also had an experimental trap door that fitted over the stairs. Braking equipment on all ten cars consisted of magnetic, hand-wheel and hand-track. Coincidentally, this batch included Bournemouth's 'Last Tram', No 7, and Llandudno's 'Last Tram', No 8.

Nos 23 and 24: ex-Darwen cars

The last additions to the fleet were acquired from Darwen in 1946. These two all-metal-bodied streamlined double-deck trams were built in 1936 by English Electric at Preston and had cost £2,750 each when new; the

Ex-Darwen streamlined tram No 23 of 1946. *R. B. Parr, NTM*

L&CBER snapped them up for £400 each, including spare parts still held at Darwen.

They had centre entrances, enclosed drivers' cabins and accommodation for 56 passengers on two-and-one transverse upholstered seats with the exception of a bench seat facing the stairs in each saloon. Re-painted in the L&CBER livery of green and cream, the fleet numbers were unintentionally transposed - No 23 becoming No 24 and vice versa.

The cars were mounted on English Electric maximum-traction bogie trucks with roller bearings, and these were equipped with one type EE305A 57 hp motor per bogie. Braking was by hand-wheel and air-wheel. An emergency air brake lever was also located near the entrance/exit doors for operation by the conductor if required. The bogies were sent to Messrs E. E. Baguley, an engineering firm in Burton-on-Trent, for regauging from 4 ft 0 in to 3 ft 6 in, and did not arrive in Llandudno until September 1947, which delayed their appearance on the Llandudno tracks.

Air hooters were fitted instead of the more usual foot-operated gongs. Dewirement indicators were fitted to both driving cabs and local destinations were added to the existing screens fitted to the front and rear of the tram (four per car). Different on each car, both included the through terminal points, No 23 also showing the local points in Llandudno and No 24 the local points for the Colwyn Bay section, plus 'PRIVATE CAR', 'DEPOT' and blank. The two indicator boxes above the entrance doors do not appear to have been fitted with any screens at all during their life at Llandudno.

Works cars

Purchased from the Leamington & Warwick Tramways in 1930 (fleet number unconfirmed as 11), the first works car had been built by Brush as a four-window open-top car, mounted on a Brush truck with a 6 ft 0 in wheelbase. Originating from the Taunton tramway (fleet number unknown), it was converted to a 'scrubber car' at Leamington and continued in that roll in Llandudno where it was numbered 23 and painted grey.

This works car was replaced in 1936 by the arrival of ex-Bournemouth No 55 dating from 1901. Constructed by G. F. Milnes for the Poole & District Electric Traction Co, it was mounted on a Brill 6 ft 6 in wheelbase four-wheel truck. It was converted to a rail grinder for use on the Bournemouth tramways, and although all upper-deck fittings were removed, it retained its direct spiral stairs fitted to tubular newel posts. Painted grey, it assumed the number 23, replacing the previous works car. When toast-rack 19 was re-numbered 23 in 1936, the works car became 23A, but reverted to 23 when the toast-rack was altered back to 19 during the winter of 1937-38. With the arrival of the two ex-Darwen trams, the works car was given the number 23A permanently.

The original ex-Leamington works car, having been stored on a short siding in the front of the depot, was eventually moved to the rear of the field adjacent to the main depot, where its windows were sheeted over with corrugated iron and its platforms removed. It became a store and survived until at least April 1957.

Other moveable items of rolling-stock over the years included a horse-drawn tower wagon and a pair of four-wheel low-sided wagons that used to be parked on a siding on Penrhyn Hill, and which were propelled in front of a tram to West Shore Parade to collect and transport sand back to the depot for drying out prior to being used in the trams. There were also two hand-propelled tower wagons, one of which lived in the depot, the other in the Llandudno Council yard at the rear of the Town Hall; their purpose was to ensure reasonably quick access to an overhead problem at either end of the route.

The tower was later removed from the horse-drawn chassis and mounted on the back of a Morris light lorry. This in turn was replaced by a Ford Thames lorry, the tower being transferred to the newer vehicle.

Also on site were a pair of ex-Coventry steam tram trailer bogies, which, when coupled together, were used for the transporting of lengths of rail. In addition there was a small four-wheel hand-propelled trolley that lived in the depot and was used for transferring heavy items from one part of the shed to another. This remained until the 'Red' buses ceased operations in May 1961, having made several unscheduled passenger trips up and down the tracks of No 2 road the month before!

Above The terminus at West Shore could be a bleak spot due to its exposed position on the Conway estuary. there are not many passengers for No 8 as her driver awaits the signal from his conductor to start the journey to Colwyn Bay. *Photographer unknown*

TO COLWYN BAY 👉

Above right Passengers make their way to their seats on the top deck to enjoy a ride to Colwyn Bay on a warm, sunny day. Ahead stretches Gloddaeth Avenue, with the large Odeon cinema and Winter Gardens ballroom dominating the skyline. A Sunbeam saloon turns into Great Ormes Road. The absence of litter confirms the self-discipline that people had, and the full wire litter basket attached to the lamp-post bears testimony to that discipline. *H. B. Priestley, NTM*

Right Where Gloddaeth Avenue and Gloddaeth Street meet was what was known as Clifton Road Loop. Double-deck tram No 14 has had to wait until toast-rack No 19 clears the single-line section leading to Palladium Corner. The styles of architecture denote the different building periods and tastes around the turn of the century. The Odeon cinema dates from late 1934 and is prominent on the south side of the street in this August 1952 scene. *H. B. Priestley, NTM*

As the tram approaches the popular centre of Llandudno at Palladium Corner (this location was known by many names, but was referred to by the tramway as either Hooson's or Palladium Corner), holidaymakers are clearly visible and the flags and bunting on the Post Office and Carlton Hotel indicate that this is 1953, Coronation year. Among road vehicles visible is a Morris 14/25 Series 3 convertible and a Bradford Jowett van. The limousines double-parked in the central area are taxis (up to eight are licensed to stand there), and just beyond them a queue of passengers awaits our tram. No 12 has arrived from Colwyn Bay and unloaded her passengers, and is waiting to proceed to the West Shore. *H. B. Priestley, NTM*

Taken from a cafe window looking down on Palladium Corner along Mostyn Street, ex-Accrington tram No 1 turns into the town's main shopping thoroughfare, pausing briefly to allow a lady to use the zebra crossing. Note the row of glazed canopies above the pavements affording pedestrians ample cover in wet weather, and also the small Ford van with advertising boards fixed to its sides. Not much other traffic is in evidence in this late afternoon shot taken on 13 May 1955.

In the comparison view taken in June 1996, the roundabout and kerb walling are the most obvious additions, and alterations have taken place to many shop fronts. There are more vehicles to be seen and a Mk 2 Leyland National bus (HWA 571), belonging to Alpine Bus, now a subsidiary of Crosville Wales, turns into Gloddaeth Street on service 16 to Conway Morfa. *A. D. Packer/author*

Above Another busy scene at Palladium Corner, with two ex-Accrington cars having arrived together at the end of Gloddaeth Street, while ex-Bournemouth No 15 loads prior to departing for Colwyn Bay. The duty Inspector is making sure that all the passengers can get on board the leading tram as it is working the Llandudno 'local' service; that will enable the following tram to reverse quickly at West Shore and catch up its time. To the right of No 15 is a splendid building that is partly occupied by leading fashion house Marie et Cie; this used to advertise above its entrance the words 'By appointment to Her Majesty the Queen of Roumania', reminding townsfolk and visitors of her five-week stay in the town in 1890. As an author she wrote under the pen-name of Carmen Sylva, but appears never to have referred to Llandudno in her writings. Streets were named after her in the eastern suburb of Craig-y-Don, and a number of local shops boasted of her patronage for years after her departure. *D. W. K. Jones, NTM*

Below A dull day on Mostyn Street as ex-Accrington tram No 4 makes her way along the single line section. A few houses on the lower slopes of the Great Orme can also be seen. To the left, on the corner of Lloyd Street, the Union & Conservative club has its rooms. Mr Hamilton, the tramway Manager, was a member there and it was not unknown for him to come out in the evening and stop a passing tram to obtain £1 from the conductor's bag, leaving the conductor with his personal IOU to be balanced the following day when his cash was counted. *A. D. Packer*

Opposite page Ex-Bournemouth trams Nos 7 and 8 meet at the busy intersection at the end of Mostyn Street and the commencement of Mostyn Broadway on 26 August 1953. As passengers board and climb to the upper deck of No 7, an Inspector assists passengers to alight on the opposite side of the road. The Crosville bus seen between the two trams is a Leyland 'chassisless' with a Beadle body, one of a handful of vehicles built to conform with a maximum weight limit for buses crossing the Conway suspension bridge on the A55 into Conway.

Comparing the 1996 photograph with the previous one, the principal differences are the one-way system and 'traffic-calming' measures that have been introduced. The Lunt sisters have moved on and their shop is now occupied by 'Butterfly'; the Broadway Hotel retains its character, but the former North Western Hotel to the right has changed its name to The Tudno Castle Hotel. *R. B. Parr, NTM/Stuart A. Rivers*

Above left On Mostyn Broadway toast-rack tram No 21 approaches the crossover that was installed in 1954. Note the gas lamp with its tapered base, and the ornamental base at the foot of the traction pole. These additions were common on most tramway systems, many poles featuring elaborate embellishments and incorporating civic emblems; their lesser-known role was to minimise the effects of dogs' urine on the bases! It is recorded that one undertaking, when deciding how tall the protective cover should be, debated the height and trajectories of water that was likely to be distributed by various breeds of dog! *H. B. Priestley, NTM*

Left The bad state of the roadway and tram track on Mostyn Broadway can be clearly seen in this 1955 view as ex-Bournemouth tram No 13 passes the small Llandudno Town depot of Crosville. Beyond the depot is the Grand Theatre, opened in 1901 and taken over during the Second World War by the BBC Variety Department, which had been evacuated from London. A regular series of variety shows was broadcast from here, and introduced as 'coming to you from somewhere in Britain'.

Inspector Ernie Woolley and his wife were present at one of these concerts, and so was a conductor, sitting a couple of rows in front of them. The snag was that the conductor was supposed to be on 'jumper duty' in Llandudno at the time. He did not know that his boss was seated almost behind him, but he did next day when he was suspended from duty without pay for a couple of days. . . *John Fozard*

This page On a sunny afternoon in May 1955 ex-Accrington tram

No 3 is seen on Mostyn Broadway heading towards the Grand Theatre and Craig-y-Don. The Arcadia Theatre, famous for its 'Catlin Follies' summer shows widely advertised on the front of the trams, can be seen on the left, and there are two Crosville buses parked adjacent to their depot obscured by the tram.

In the similar view taken in September 1996 the Grand Theatre is visible, and so too is part of the now doomed Arcadia Theatre. The once open spaces have all but vanished under car parks and a new theatre and conference complex fronting the promenade. A petrol station now occupies the site of Crosville's former Llandudno Town depot. *A. D. Packer/Stuart A. Rivers*

Left This was the view that greeted passengers travelling on the top deck when their tram reached the end of Mostyn Avenue in Craig-y-Don. The tram would cross Nant-y-Gamar Road and enter the Bodafon Fields, making its way towards Craigside and the climb up to the top of Penrhyn Hill. The Little Orme forms the background and the houses at Craigside are visible on this sunny morning in August 1954. The crops in the fields are ripening as ex-Accrington tram No 5 approaches the tram stop at Nant-y-Gamar Road. A notice board reminds the public that the tramline here is a private right-of-way. It was not unknown for motorists, when following a tram home in thick fog at night, to drive into the fields until the somewhat rough ride that developed made them reconsider their position! *H. B. Priestley, NTM*

Below left Trackwork is receiving attention in the small cutting on the Bodafon Fields, three workmen being engaged on repacking the concrete sleepers on 27 August 1953. Driver Eric Isles slows toast-rack No 22 as he prepares to pass the group on his journey towards Colwyn Bay. The tram carries a full complement of holidaymakers. *H. B. Priestley, NTM*

Above right An unusual scene of a Llandudno tram in the snow, as original 1907 car No 17 hurries through the Bodafon Fields towards Craigside. Being so close to the sea the snow does not stick for long, but in the winter of 1954 this photographer was able to get his picture before the last traces had melted. *H. Moore*

Below Maintenance on the reserved track sections did not stop at track, poles and wires, but included the pruning of bushes and the cutting down of long grass and brambles where they were likely to interfere with the passing trams. Seen near Craigside curve in the Bodafon Fields, ex-Bournemouth car No 14, driven by Bobby Williams, passes Geoff Bird, carrying a hand sickle, making his way back to the tower wagon that has been parked beyond the tram. The distinctive features of the Great Orme can be seen in the background. *A. D. Packer*

As our tram climbs towards Penrhyn Hill in May 1954, ex-Bournemouth car No 15 glides into view and prepares to pick up the lady waiting at Craigside halt. A public footpath crosses the track here and its stile can be seen on the right. The lamp on the pole was usually switched on at dusk by the tram conductors, and the crew of the last tram at night going back to the depot would ensure that it was switched off. There were several of these lamps at the stops on the company's private roads. *H. B. Priestley, NTM*

Above A lovely summer view taken near the top of the Bodafon Fields in 1946. With the hedgerows full of their summer flowers you can almost feel the warmth and hear the bees and crickets at work. Only the background whine of No 17's motors breaks the quiet of an otherwise peaceful summer day. *S. H. Keyso, courtesy of O. H. Prosser*

Below Back to School! Local schools in North Wales begin their Autumn term earlier than their English counterparts, and this interesting scene taken on 29 August 1954 shows three school-children on their bicycles, no doubt racing each other down Bryn-y-Bia Road; they have had to swerve to avoid ex-Bournemouth tram No 7, which has just emerged from the fields, only to have to swerve again to avoid a photographer standing in the middle of the road recording the event! *A. D. Packer*

Above The track looked a bit like a 'switchback' on Bryn-y-Bia Road, and ex-Accrington tram No 1 has been photographed from an outcrop of rock, showing the tram track, laid in granite setts (the only stretch of line to be paved in this way) undulating with the contours of the road. The fast descent towards Llandudno was quite exhilarating, especially on board a toast-rack. Notice boards attached to several poles along this section of line (one is visible) reminded the public that the Light Railway was private property and did not constitute a public right-of-way. Perhaps that is why it was paved differently from the other part of the road. *D. W. K. Jones, NTM*

Below A later view of ex-Accrington No 1 pausing at the compulsory stop at the top of Penrhyn Hill, as a Crosville bus disappears down the gradient towards Llandudno. The large advertising board on the right has its words picked out with reflective glass studs, so that at night headlights from vehicles climbing Penrhyn Hill would be able to pick out its message quite clearly. The board on the wall of the public conveniences on the left directs people along a minor lane to the village of Penrhynside. It is 20 April 1955, and the buds are just beginning to break on the trees. *H. B. Priestley, NTM*

This photograph does not do justice to the steep and difficult road junction at the top of Penrhyn Hill. An unidentified ex-Bournemouth tram emerges from its reserved track and the climb up the hill from the Little Orme Cafe, to cross the busy A546 road on 29 August 1953. The Crosville bus driver will be hoping he does not have to stop before the tram moves out of his way. *R. B. Parr, NTM*

Above Ex-Accrington tram No 4 descends Penrhyn Hill on a May morning in 1955. The tram track here was on a shelf cut out from the side of the hill, the main A546 road dipping away on the left. At its steepest point the gradient was 1:11; tram drivers had to descend with caution, and conductors were supposed to be on the rear platform holding the trolley rope in case of dewirement. Some drivers were able to lock on just enough handbrake to enable a controlled descent, the tram pulling up exactly at the Little Orme Cafe stop at the foot of the hill. *M. J. O'Connor, NTM*

Below Looking down Penrhyn Hill towards the Little Orme Cafe and the commencement of Glan-y-Mor Road, ex-Bournemouth

car No 13 is seen approaching an occupation crossing that used to lead around the Little Orme to the quarry that is situated on its seaward side. The quarry was worked between circa 1890 and 1931 and contributed to the early development of Penrhyn Bay as its workers found housing close to their work. The advent of the tramway accelerated the development of property along its line of route, and the terraced properties known as Quarry Cottages still exist at the Glan-y-Mor Road end of Maesgwyn Road. To the left of this picture, taken in June 1954, there used to be a small quarry owned by the tram company, which included a short siding connected to the down line of the tramway. *R. J. S. Wiseman*

Above Ex-Bournemouth tram No 6 pulls away from the Little Orme Cafe at the foot of Penrhyn Hill, along Glan-y-Mor Road towards Penrhyn Bay. Note the small timber shelter, white enamel 'request' tram stop plate and the pole-mounted light. The field to the left of this view has since been developed into an extensive private housing estate. *H. B. Priestley, NTM*

Below Sweeping around St David's Corner, ex-Bournemouth tram No 8 enters the unmade section the company-owned Glan-y-Mor Road with a full load of passengers on 13 August 1954. To the right, but out of view, is a bungalow whose owner published a book about his dog 'Sandy', a golden labrador. The houses up in Penrhynside village are visible beyond the hedge on the right of the picture. *H. B. Priestley, NTM*

Above In 1952 development had started on the remaining land between St David's Corner and Benarth Road along Glan-y-Mor Road. Ex-Bournemouth tram No 10 heads towards the sea at Penrhyn Bay, passing the home of General Manager W. G. Hamilton, who had a tram stop especially sited opposite his home (second pole down). The majority of the lattice traction poles seen here were replaced a year later by tubular poles and span-wire construction. *H. B. Priestley, NTM*

Below Driver Les Owen brings ex-Accrington tram No 4 to a halt

at the Benarth Road stop. The unmade state of the road can be seen, and it was to remain in this condition until it was purchased by the local authority in 1963 and properly adopted, being made up the following year. The small shelter on the left was one of two comprising seven vestibule doors from the scrapped 1907 trams, the other being sited at St David's Corner. *M. J. O'Connor, NTM*

Above right Midsummer's evening, 21 June 1945, and two well-patronised ex-Bournemouth trams, Nos 7 and 8, pass near Maesgwyn Road, Penrhyn Bay. The top-deck light has been removed from No 8, probably as a wartime precaution, and the addition of a box containing a small red light attached to the left-hand windscreen can also be seen. The sea is almost dead calm, but there must have been a chill in the air because everybody on the photograph is well wrapped up, including the photographer's mother who is occupying the seaside bench visible between the trams. The rooftops and houses at Rhos-on-Sea are visible in the distance. *E. C. Haywood*

Right Breaches in the sea wall at Penrhyn Bay got progressively worse, forcing the tram company to operate a single line past the problem, which became permanent from 1952. On 13 August 1954 it is clear where the seaward track has been undermined and partially re-filled in an attempt to lessen the effects, or at least to try and slow down what seemed to be the inevitable and ultimate destruction of the tram track. The site interests the two gentlemen in the foreground, and it has not escaped the attention of passengers on the tram. *H. B. Priestley, NTM*

In 1952 the track on the right is slowly being reclaimed by the beach as ex-Bournemouth tram No 14 rolls down the gentle gradient towards the Golf House. The replacement tubular poles and bracket arms are visible, and the seaward overhead wire has been realigned to follow more closely the running line in the direction of Colwyn Bay. The second photograph shows the scene today about 100 yards away from the previous one, and shows the promenade and sea wall near the junction with Marine Drive and Morfa Road. *E. C. Haywood/ Stuart A. Rivers*

Above This interesting view taken on 27 July 1948 is looking towards Rhos-on-Sea, showing the Marine Drive and toll gate. The original limestone wall protecting the land from the sea also shelters the little toll house, adjacent to which an anemometer is mounted on top of the traction pole. A fully-laden ex-Bournemouth tram heads toward Rhos, while an Armstrong Siddeley can be seen in the Golf Club car park. *H. B. Priestley, NTM*

Below The conductor of ex-Accrington tram No 2 is having difficulty in the wind with his trolley-rope, although why the trolley is on the wrong wire is a mystery. The toll house and keeper can be seen on the left; the toll keeper was former tram Inspector Nat Chadderton. He had joined the company in 1907 as one of its first employees and was to remain at his post at the tollgate until it was auctioned late in 1962. Interviewed in the national press at the time under the headline 'Britain's oldest Toll Collector' (he was then 87 years old), he was asked what he would be doing when the road was sold. With a twinkle in his eye, he replied, 'I'll just look for another job!' Motorists who were caught unawares by the toll road would either pay up or panic. When approached by Nat, the panickers would ask feebly, 'How do I get out of this?', to which the reply in sardonic tones was, 'The same way as you came, laddy, the same way as you came.' Nat Chadderton died peacefully on 17 July 1970 aged 94. *H. B. Priestley, NTM*

Eric Old

Above Viewed from the bedroom window of a property fronting Marine Drive, Penrhyn Bay, ex-Bournemouth tram No 8 is seen heading toward Orme Point in April 1955. New sea defence work is well in hand, agreement having been reached with all frontagers (including the tramway company, which owned a long length of the road) as to the level of financial contribution each would make towards the project. The bulk of the funding came from Central Government for sea-defence works. *H. B. Priestley, NTM*

Below Photographed from the top deck of a tram standing in the depot yard, ex-Bournemouth tram No 11 is seen approaching the Church Road stop in Penrhyn Avenue. The Little Orme is just visible in the background behind the houses at Orme Point. *M. J. O'Connor, NTM*

On an August afternoon in 1954 ex-Bournemouth tram No 6 pauses briefly at the Request stop adjacent to the Colwyn Bay Cricket Club. Passengers on the top deck are looking at the match in play, one of many played during the club's annual Cricket Festival. Some of the spectators can be seen over the fence, together with an invalid car whose occupant is getting a good view of the game. Cars on Penrhyn Avenue include two Fords, one Morris and a Hillman Minx Phase 1. *H. B. Priestley, NTM*

Above Following the end of the summer season in 1948, the tram company opened up part of Penrhyn Avenue near the cricket ground to relay some of its tram track utilising timber sleepers (the opposite track was laid on concrete sleepers.) Single-line operation took place between the crossover outside the tram depot and the points in the photograph near Colwyn Crescent. Ex-Bournemouth tram No 9 is seen passing the newly relaid section in October 1948. *F. E. J. Ward*

Below Herbert Pitman brings toast-rack No 22 along Penrhyn Avenue towards the Promenade at Rhos-on-Sea on 13 August 1954. The Llandudno-bound track assumes a gutter-running position just where the Ford car can be seen. The rear boot encasing the spare wheel on the car to the left is an interesting feature. A lorry driver, making a local delivery, is just visible beyond. *H. B. Priestley, NTM*

Above Ex-Accrington tram No 4 approaches the Promenade at Rhos-on-Sea and passes the Rhos Playhouse cinema on Penrhyn Avenue. The building is now in use as a Co-op 'Stop 'n' Shop' grocers, while the land to the left of the building was being developed in September 1996. The building in the background was demolished and the site that extends around the corner on to the Promenade has been extensively redeveloped. *A. D. Packer*

Below When photographed on 28 May 1946 on the Promenade at Rhos-on-Sea, 1907 tram No 17 was looking decidedly weary and in need of a fresh coat of paint. The black sign with the white 'S' mounted on the traction pole on the right directs people to an air-raid shelter; a left-over from the war, somebody has forgotten to remove it! The notice board below advertises free admission to a local show. *E. C. Haywood, courtesy of R. Meadowcroft*

Fully laden ex-Bournemouth tram No 7 bites into the reverse curves leading from Rhos Promenade up on to the short Caley Promenade on 22 August 1952. Lots of day-trippers and holidaymakers contribute to make this picture full of life. A Ford Pilot and part of an Austin pick-up are visible, and there is even a public weighing machine attached to the lamp standard in the centre of the picture. *H. B. Priestley, NTM*

Above Ex-Darwen tram No 24 working on the Colwyn Bay 'local' was caught by the camera on the Caley Promenade just below the Mount Stewart Hotel in 1953. One night at this location an ex-Bournemouth tram proceeding towards Colwyn Bay suffered a dewirement for no apparent reason. The conductor got out and put the trolley back on the wire, but the lights in the tram did not go back on, and after trying various switches the crew deduced that there must have been a power failure, so they just sat there and waited. Eventually a tram came from the Colwyn Bay direction, so the power must have been on. The conductor got out and checked the trolley again and found that in the darkness he had somehow put it on one of the insulated span wires instead, so it was hardly surprising that there was no power! The tram was now about 15 minutes late, and as the driver was a cautious fellow, the time was never caught up and the tram ran late for the rest of the night! *N. P. Willis, NTM*

Below Brompton Avenue formed part of the main A546 road between Colwyn Bay and Llandudno, and as such the road surface, at least on the stretch used by the trams, was always in good condition. Ex-Bournemouth tram No 12 approaches the top of the hill on 14 May 1955, ready to make a sharp right-hand turn on to the narrow bridge crossing the main Chester-Holyhead railway line - a 'Road Narrows' sign warns motorists of the hazard. A magnificent Rolls-Royce has pulled up at the stop line at the end of Llanerch Road East. In the background the glazed red-brick Hermon Eglwys Brestbyteraidd Cymru Church, built in 1903, dominates the corner. *A. D. Packer*

Above Once on the bridge, the trams took up a central position and traffic not familiar with the road tended to follow the tram across. There were exceptions of course - one afternoon a coach coming from the Llandudno direction turned on to the bridge, cutting the corner as he did so, only to see to his horror a double-deck tram right in front of him. He tried to squeeze past, but although the tram managed to stop, the bus did not. As a result several rear panels of the coach were ripped off, although the tram was barely scratched. After exchanging details, the tram continued on its way, the coach driver being left to stow the twist-ed and torn body panels in his rear luggage compartment! In this picture, taken on 1 June 1955, a Triumph Mayflower follows ex-Accrington tram No 5 at a safe distance!

The properties immediately to the left of the tram have since been demolished to make way for a new and realigned bridge at this location, which was brought about as part of the construction of the new A55 coastal Expressway in the 1980s. At the same time the four-track railway that passed beneath the bridge was reduced to two lines and the trackbed realigned as extra land was purchased to make way for the new trunk road. *M. J. O'Connor, NTM*

Opposite page When originally opened in 1876, the old 'Board School', which forms the backdrop to this 1956 view, stood in splendid isolation at the junction of the roads to Conway and Llandudno, and the nearby fields were used for cricket and football. It was felt that being so far out of Colwyn Bay, the pupils would benefit from the fresh air. Eighty years later the situation had changed, and the school was surrounded by development that now comprises the West End of Colwyn Bay. Its front boundary wall was moved back in 1931 in conjunction with the road widening that was then taking place. At the same time, at the request of the local police, the junction was modified and a short length of dual carriageway together with a small traffic island were installed. These can be seen here, together with ex-Bournemouth tram No 14 about to turn on to Conway Road towards Colwyn Bay. Pupils attending the school can recall how the teachers would pause every 20 minutes or so in the winter (more often in the summer) whenever a tramcar passed by outside, as the noise drowned the sound of their voices!

At the same location 40 years on again, the major change has been brought about by the construction of the A55 Expressway, opened in 1985. The demolition of the former Brompton Avenue bridge to make way for a new one on a different alignment means that the school now has a new and superelevated road junction in front of it. *Brian P. Martin, courtesy of Martin Jenkins/Stuart A. Rivers*

West End, Colwyn Bay, showing the main A55 Conway Road: to the left is a No 1-type telephone box introduced in 1921, glazed on three sides and with a glazed timber door. A Ford Popular chases ex-Accrington tram No 2 towards town. Seen from the top deck of a tram, part of the Council school is visible on the right-hand side of the road.

H. B. Priestley, NTM

Above 1907 tram No 17 is seen on Conway Road, approaching Marine Road, as a Ford van heads towards West End. The very large gas lamps fitted to the tram standards in Colwyn Bay were most distinctive and reflected quite a bright light at night. They could be seen between West End and the Council Offices at Coed Pellar Road. There were also a couple located at Rhos-on-Sea in Penrhyn Avenue near the Promenade. The Compulsory tram stop on the left served the Odeon cinema (not visible) and, accordingly, a timetable case was provided below it for intending passengers to peruse. *A. D. Packer*

Below On 25 September 1955 ex-Accrington tram No 3 and a Ford V8 Pilot towing a caravan pass the Odeon Cinema at the corner of Marine Road. The cinema, designed by company architect Harry Weedon, opened in 1936 with two performances each night, three on Saturdays but none on Sundays. So much traffic congestion was caused by patrons parking on all the main roads and side roads that the tram and bus stops were moved on several occasions under direction of the local police.

The Odeon chain was founded in 1930 by Oscar Deutsch, who endeavoured to put an Odeon cinema in the High Street of every town in the country with a population of over 25,000. The name was said to derive from 'Oscar Deutsch Entertains Our Nation'. This Odeon closed in 1957, was re-opened as the Astra in 1969 but finally closed in 1986 and was demolished a year later. Swn-y-Mor retirement apartments now occupy the site. *R. J. S. Wiseman*

Above Between Coed Pellar Road and Woodland Road West, Conway Road was particularly narrow; indeed, it was considered too narrow for a double tram track, so in 1929, when the road was redeveloped, a length of interlaced track was provided for the trams. Here ex-Bournemouth tram No 13 enters the section from the Llandudno direction behind a light van. There is a workman on the right standing on an unprotected ladder attending to a problem on the glazed cast-iron canopy roof. One of the large ornamental street lamp bases is visible in the foreground bearing the arms of Colwyn Bay Council together with other ornate embellishments. *Eric Thornton*

Below Another landmark that has been swept away in the name of progress is the fountain that once stood at the top of Station Road, Colwyn Bay. It had been presented to the town in 1895 by Mr John Porter, one of the town's pioneers, and was removed in 1959 when, due to serious traffic congestion, a one-way traffic scheme was introduced to some roads leading off Conway Road. Ex-Bournemouth tramcar No 10 is seen passing the top of Station Road, and rolling gently down to the stop opposite St Paul's Church. *A. D. Packer*

Opposite page A busy scene in the centre of Colwyn Bay in August 1954. 1907 tram No 17 is seen next to a fully laden ex-Bournemouth tramcar, behind which is an assortment of vehicles including one of only six pre-war Leyland TD5 buses belonging to Crosville, which could be converted to open-top condition during the summer months if required. These were in the Crosville fleet M71-M76 number series and were finally withdrawn in 1958. The shop blinds have been pulled out over the pavement to protect the goods in the windows from the glare of the sun.

The same view in 1996 shows dominant road traffic signs, a Crosville mini-bus and an Alpine Leyland National. Fewer shop blinds appear to be in use. Although this road still gets very busy at times, imagine what it might be like if the Expressway had not been built! Perhaps pedestrians would have been using the cars as stepping stones to cross the road. *H. B. Priestley, NTM/Stuart A. Rivers*

A morning scene taken on 28 August 1955. The bunting is celebrating the town's annual festival as John Glyn Jones brings toast-rack tram No 21 up the final rise approaching the terminus at Greenfield Road, Colwyn Bay. During one season John spent six weeks driving this type of tram, and as a result sported a suntan that could have been favourably compared with someone of Mediterranean origin! *H. B. Priestley, NTM*

Ex-Accrington tram No 2 approaches the terminal stub on Abergele Road at its junction with Greenfield Road. Following the abandonment of the tramway to Old Colwyn, the trams terminated at St Paul's Church until the terminal stub was created in the location shown in this picture. Trams resumed running through to Greenfield Road, but the police were unhappy about trams standing in the centre of the road, so they were once again relegated to St Paul's. The solution came late in 1931 when the roadway was widened on the right-hand side, which then allowed the centre line to be moved to the right also. This enabled trams to enter the terminal and be in the correct position to move off with the flow of traffic. The company then put an extra 1d stage on its fares between St Paul's and the new terminus, but following local objections this was removed after a few weeks. The shield mounted on the traction pole reads 'Trams leave here for Rhos, Penrhyn Bay, Penrhynside, Little Orme and Llandudno', and was still in situ in 1957, a year after the trams ceased to run. The Austin A40 has been parked in a thoughtless (although not illegal then) position! *H. B. Priestley, NTM*

MISCELLANY

Before we catch the tram back to Llandudno, let's take a look at a selection of miscellaneous scenes around the system.

These were the Tramway Offices in Penrhyn Avenue, which were situated on the left-hand side of the tram shed and yard. The building was originally used as a cycle and repair shop, and during the mid-1930s the large room in the middle of the building was used as an Ebenezer Mission Hall. When the religious group left, it became a workmen's club run by local brewers Ind Coope who sold their own Alsops beer. This has been affectionately known as 'All slops bitter'. The whole building was ultimately secured by the tramway for its main office block. *Brian P. Martin*

A wartime shot of original 1907 tram No 18 working the Llandudno 'local'. Taken on 29 April 1942, other wartime features in the photograph include the warning white bands painted on the electricity box mounted on the edge of the pavement and the tree trunk. The tram has its bumper painted white and the small boxes containing the small red warning lights are just visible on the windscreens. A route board is still in position on the side of the tram's roof. Beyond the tram is some sort of temporary brick building on the spot usually reserved for the little buses operating the Great Orme circular service; whatever purpose they served, they were removed soon after the war. *A. V. Mace, NTM*

In 1946 the company bought two streamlined double-deck tram-cars from Darwen in Lancashire. They were thought to be ideal for operating the winter service on the Llandudno tramway, and expectations were high when the first of the pair, No 24, arrived by road on 19 August. This tram and her sister, No 23, became the first trams to pass through the Mersey Tunnel between Liverpool and Birkenhead. When that tunnel was built it was hoped that a tramway route linking both sides of the Mersey would be built and operated below the present roadway, but in the 1930s Birkenhead adopted a conversion-to-buses policy so the idea was never developed. The two trams were eventually repainted and re-united with their bogies, which had been re-gauged by Messrs E. E. Baguley Ltd of Burton-upon-Trent in September 1947. *Photographer unknown*

Almost as soon as it has arrived at the terminus, passengers board streamline double-deck tram No 24 in Colwyn Bay while the conductor turns the trolley. Working the local service to Rhos on 24 July 1949, it would not have much standing time before it would have to be off on its return journey. Its indicators at this end show 'Colwyn Bay', while those at the other end would be showing 'Church Road'. *H. B. Priestley, NTM*

In June 1953 both streamlined double-deckers were operating on the Colwyn Bay local service. Here No 23 has entered the interlaced section on Conway Road. On the right of the tram, the English Presbyterian Church can be seen, while on the opposite corner stands Martins Bank (now Barclays). An AEC lorry and an Austin van are following the tram while a motorist driving in the opposite direction is towing a small yacht on a trailer.

The photographer was doing National Service at nearby Rhyl and used to visit the tramway every weekend while he was stationed in the area. On one such visit he boarded a tram at the top of Penrhyn Hill. When he climbed to the top deck, he was amazed to find that it was packed with friends and neighbours from his home town of Darwen who had come to the area for the day on their annual church outing and who were equally surprised to see him! *H. L. Runnett*

Above Streamlined No 24 stands at the crossover just inside the Bodafon Fields at Craig-y-Don. Photographed in August 1948, the trolley has been turned ready to cross back on to the Llandudno track. The driver's external cab door can also be seen in the open position. *A. R. Spencer*

Below Inside Rhos-on-Sea Depot in August 1956 are two of the four remaining trams, Nos 12 and 23, in the company of three buses parked in the paint shop. The tower wagon is parked alongside Mr Butterworth's car. The two other trams still on site outside in the yard were No 24 and the lower saloon of No 11 minus its vestibules. *D. W. K. Jones, NTM*

A general view of part of the depot yard at Rhos-on-Sea taken from a passing tramcar. 1907 tram No 18 is being coaxed out of the yard by a fitter while the Inspector guides the trolley. As there were no connecting junctions in the overhead wire between the 'main line' and the depot (there were six inside the depot yard leading on to the different shed roads), conductors would have to pull their trolleys down from one wire and place it on to the appropriate wire while the tram was still moving. No 6 has been prepared for a private party and behind can be seen an ex-Accrington tram and one of the ex-Darwen streamliners. Marks in the road surface bear witness to derailments that happened occasionally. *D. W. K. Jones, NTM*

Henry Priestley made a point of photographing the interiors of tramsheds, and this view at Rhos in 1949 captures a wealth of detail. The depot was simply constructed with corrugated material for the walls and roof, the latter having glazed lights set at regular intervals. A lower extension running the full width of the shed was added in the 1920s and provided much-needed additional workspace. The area to the left, behind the full-height partition, concealed the paint and joiner's shop. Directly in front, to the left of the double-deck tram, stands the portable generator and welding gear. To the rear at the right is the blacksmith's shop, while up on the wall can be seen wheels and belts to drive the wheel lathe and other items of machinery. The little works car, No 23A, usually 'lived' here on the short No 1 road. One of the streamlined double-deck trams can be seen in front of an ex-Accrington car. *H. B. Priestley, NTM*

Another interesting study inside Rhos-on-Sea Depot taken by Priestley on 10 August 1949 from inside the cab of one of the 1907 trams. Visible are a toast-rack, both ex-Darwen streamlined double-deck trams and an ex-Accrington single-decker. In the immediate foreground, the forward/reverse key on the top of the controller can be seen, as well as part of the vertically mounted handbrake wheel, which was peculiar to the 1907 trams. *H. B. Priestley, NTM*

At the rear of the depot at the end of road four, tram No 8 has been raised on jacks while work is carried out on her bogies. The date is unknown but could possibly be the autumn of 1953 when her motors and gears were substituted for equipment from Birmingham. Other assorted tackle for the lifting of heavy equipment can be seen. The gentleman in the foreground is warming himself by the blacksmith's brazier. *Photographer unknown*

Right Overhead linesmen Geoff Bird and Evan Jones pose with the company's tower wagon. The tower was originally set on a horse-drawn wagon, and prior to the acquisition of this Ford Thames lorry was fitted to an older Morris lorry around 1930. *N. P. Willis, NTM*

Below A snapshot taken circa 1950 showing the debris thrown on to the tram tracks by the sea at Penrhyn Bay during the winter gales. Although the golf course has also suffered from flooding, it would appear that the 19th hole is safe at least! For a short period passengers had to change trams and make their way through the obstruction to continue their journey on another tram. *Photographer unknown*

Above Not seen out very often by photographers was the works tram, No 23A. It was on duty in Llandudno during the winter of 1953/54 when work was being carried out on the tracks on Mostyn Broadway, and is standing on the Llandudno track outside the North Western Hotel with the welding generator unit behind it. The general state of the road can be seen to the right of the tram, and it is self-evident that the work was long overdue. *A. D. Packer*

Opposite page Both tracks on Mostyn Broadway eastwards from the North Western Hotel received attention during the early part of 1954. Here the Colwyn Bay track has been opened up as far as Tudor Road; the works tram is parked at the far end. At night red oil lamps, placed alongside the open area of the road, would warn motorists of the danger; these lamps were filled with paraffin and checked daily, and a workman would ensure that all were lit before nightfall. While these works were being carried out, trams ran 'wrong line' between the library on Mostyn Street and the newly installed crossover near Tudor Road.

Viewed from a similar position in 1996 it can be seen that the width of the road has been artificially narrowed by the creation of a one-way traffic scheme, which has allowed an increase in the numbers of cars that can be parked side by side at right-angles to the kerb instead of parallel to the gutter. *A. D. Packer/Stuart A. Rivers*

In Coronation year, 1953, Reg Johnson poses with decorated tram No 13 on Rhos-on-Sea Promenade. When the late Mr P. W. Lawson (Superintendent of the Birmingham Corporation Tramway workshops) was visiting Rhos-on-Sea Depot with his son, the late Roger Lawson, to discuss the sale of Birmingham tramway equipment to the L&CBER, he enquired why a tram had not been decorated. He was told that the company did not have the time to deal with such things when there were more important matters to be dealt with. However, they were both told that if they wished to do something themselves, they were welcome to try. The Lawsons selected the most respectable looking tram in the shed and set to work. With the aid of some bunting and flags found in the depot, they produced their own version of a decorated tram, thus ensuring a contribution by the L&CBER to the general mood of Coronation year, albeit courtesy of Birmingham Tramways! *S. E. Letts*

An unusual reminder of the tramway can be found at the Rhos-on-Sea Golf Club in the form of its Challenge Trophy, presented to the club by the tramway in 1913. Pictured here with the cup is Mr F. E. Woolley, President of the Club and son of the late Mr J. E. Woolley, who was formerly Chief Inspector on the tramway. The first winner in the 1913/14 season was G. H. Goldsmith Esq. Rhos-on-Sea Golf Club is privately owned, currently by the Lythgoe family who have had it for about 30 years. It will attain its first century in 1999.

The cup is currently used as the Captain's Day Trophy. The close-up view shows the inscription on the cup, bearing testimony to its tramway roots. *Both author*

Left Members of the Manchester Model Railway Society enjoyed a 'farewell' tour of the line in the late summer of 1955. Member George Oakley, seen at the controls next to manager Walter Butterworth, had organised the event. George's wife Joan and son Rodney are to the right of Mr Butterworth, while the Chairman of the MMRS, the late Les Young, stands by the tram. The trip began at the North Western Hotel and included a visit to the depot at Rhos-on-Sea. During part of the journey George was allowed to take the controls under the supervision of the manager. George's fondness for the line is well known in tramway circles. He has a ⅝ inch to 1 foot scale model tram line in his garden, which includes

a model of each type of tram that ran on the L&CBER in addition to three models of trams from his native Manchester system. *Photographer unknown*

Below left A small group of tram enthusiasts stand beside No 10 at the occupation crossing near the foot of Penrhyn Hill on 13 May 1946. It is thought to be the first time members of the Light Railway Transport League had chartered their own tram for a tour of this line. The group, who were from the Merseyside area, enjoyed the added bonus of a sunny day. *Photographer unknown*

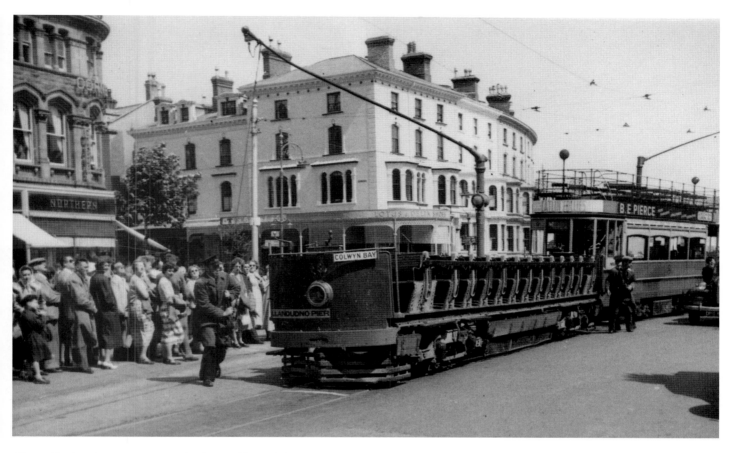

Above During the summer months the problem of time-keeping became particularly difficult if large numbers of people wanted to ride on the trams. Heavy traffic, particularly in Colwyn Bay, would cause additional delays. A basic timetable with a headway of either 10 or 15 minutes would be operated in the main part of the season, requiring eight or five trams respectively. These would be heavily duplicated by others running in between the service trams in addition to the trams operating the local shuttle service at each end of the route. Duty Inspectors

had to have their wits about them, and it was not unusual to see trams 'turned short' at Palladium Corner to ease pressure on the service cars. Often, in fine weather, toast-racks would be used as the service cars during the day, being exchanged for another tram during the evening to continue through to the close of service. Here toast-rack tram No 19 is being prepared for a quick turn-round to load up the waiting passengers and minimise the delay caused to the service tram behind. *Photographer unknown*

Above Chief Inspector Ernie Woolley has a word with the driver of ex-Bournemouth tram No 9 as it leaves the Colwyn Bay terminus on a particularly wet 6 June 1953; it is hardly surprising that there are no passengers on its upper deck. No 9 looks particularly clean and much bodywork detail can be seen. The photograph was taken from a 'special car' chartered by members of the Light Railway Transport League for their tour of the line that year. *R. J. S. Wiseman*

TO LLANDUDNO 👉

Above right Off again! After a quick turn-round, ex-Bournemouth tram No 12 leaves the terminus and heads towards its first stop at St Paul's Church, Colwyn Bay. The single-blade of the points shows up well; it used to make a hollow 'clock-clock' sound as the tram wheels passed over it and it sprang back to its pre-set position. Traffic is already causing problems along this stretch of Abergele Road. *H. B. Priestley, NTM*

Right Driver Emrys Pugh leans against his tram eating from a bag of crisps while a conductor from another tram sits on the step behind him. This scene outside St Paul's Church on Abergele Road was captured on 9 August 1947 when a short interruption of the power supply had brought the trams to a standstill. Other road vehicles have managed to get past the trams and a police sergeant on the right keeps an eye on the proceedings. *H. B. Priestley, NTM*

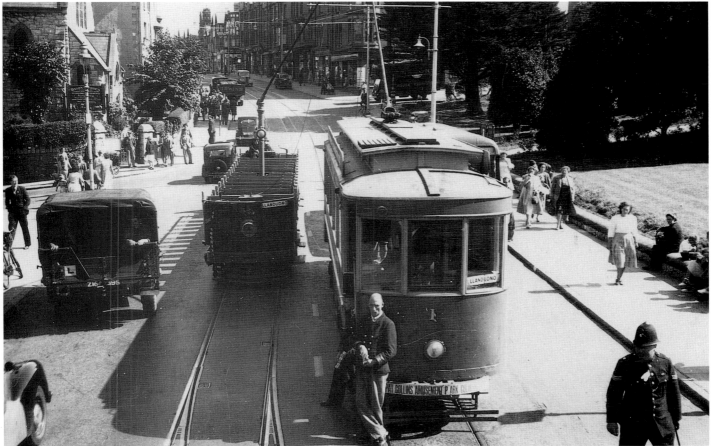

Opposite page A view full of atmosphere, taken looking towards the tram stop at St Paul's Church on 18 April 1955. Dominating the picture is an Austin Somerset and, in the distance, other cars pass ex-Bournemouth tram No 8 and a Crosville Lodekka bus. The bicycle, correctly parked against the kerb, is something not seen today; left like that now it would probably be stolen while its owner was inside a shop! Leading-name stores include F. W. Woolworth, Stead & Simpson (shoes) and Hepworths (men's outfitters). On the opposite side of the road is a branch of Melias, the Liverpool-based grocery chain. The overhead feeders providing power to the tram wires can also be seen. Ivy Street power station was located immediately behind the shops with the tall chimneys.

In 1996 there is very little change to the overall scene. A coffee bar has replaced the shoe shop and a winter sports shop occupies the former grocery shop. The bus is operating on the X8 Southport-Liverpool-Chester-Llandudno service. *H. B. Priestley, NTM/ Stuart A. Rivers*

Right Perfectly illustrating the interlaced track on Conway Road, a toast-rack tram with its fleet number missing, driven by William Arthur Jones, makes its way from the centre of Colwyn Bay towards Llandudno on 29 July 1948. This busy scene includes pedestrians, cyclists and other road vehicles, while in the far distance a pre-war Crosville TD1 loads its passengers near Station Road. *H. B. Priestley, NTM*

Below An interesting view taken on 28 August 1955 from the top deck of a tram as it proceeds towards West End. The people enjoying the seat on the left are sitting in front of the Council Offices. The spire of St John's Methodist Church can be seen beyond the large and distinctive gas lamp mounted on the traction pole. The arcade of shops on the right includes booking offices for Crosville Motor Services Ltd. Ex-Bournemouth tram No 13 approaches from West End. *M. J. O'Connor, NTM*

Above Invariably there was a build-up of traffic behind the trams when they took on passengers at the Council Offices. Here ex-Bournemouth tram No 8 has moved away from the stop followed by a procession of traffic on 4 August 1955. The Crosville bus going in the opposite direction is a Bristol Lodekka (RFM 416), new the previous year and working the 408 service to Penmaen Head. The large rear destination screens were a considerable help to the public, particularly if the bus moved off before you reached the stop - at least you could see which service you had missed. *J. J. W. Richards, NTM*

Below Original 1907 tram No 17 stops to set down a policeman and allow a lady to board in Conway Road near its junction with Alexandra Road. A lorry carrying Corona fizzy drinks, advertised as 'Britain's best beverage', overtakes on the offside of the tram. Also shown is one of the cast iron bus stops featuring the Oak Tree emblem of Colwyn Bay. These and tram stops of a similar style could be seen throughout the Colwyn Bay area. *A. D. Packer*

This is the shopping arcade at West End, Colwyn Bay, on 19 April 1955 as ex-Accrington tram No 1 glides round the gentle curve and prepares to climb the slight rise to Brompton Avenue bridge. A Triumph Roadster, an A35, a Ford Popular, a Triumph Renown and a Morris Minor are all clearly visible. *H. B. Priestley, NTM*

Above The problems of other traffic facing oncoming trams on Brompton Avenue bridge are obvious in this view, looking south and showing a Llandudno-bound tram. There was more than one occasion when motorists cut the corner only to narrowly miss or actually collide with a tram as they tried to squeeze past on the left-hand side. The Vauxhall Wyvern has no such problems in this scene, taken in the late afternoon on 16 August 1954. Also visible rising above both sides of the bridge are the telegraph poles that carried the railway signal telegraphs under the bridge to avoid the overhead wires of the tramway. Note the old 'School' road sign with its 'flaming torch' symbol. This bridge was demolished in 1985 and completely rebuilt and re-aligned. *H. B. Priestley, NTM*

Below Seen from a tram descending Brompton Avenue from the railway bridge on 26 June 1955, ex-Bournemouth tram No 9 is passing the junction of Llanerch Road East. Note the tramway pole with its bracket arm and ornate iron work, and the street gas lamps. The small road works on the left are protected by two small red flags on iron poles driven into the asphalt. Driver Les Owen adopts a relaxed pose as his tram drifts uphill towards the bridge. *M. J. O'Connor, NTM*

Above Ex-Accrington tram No 3 is about to turn into Whitehall Road from Brompton Avenue on 4 May 1955. A roundabout now occupies the centre of this road junction. *J. J. W. Richards, NTM*

Below The gently curving Whitehall Road leads the traveller to the Caley Promenade at Rhos-on-Sea, from which direction No 11 approaches with a full complement of passengers on board. *M. J. O'Connor, NTM*

Left Toast-rack No 20, lightly loaded, rounds the Mount Stewart Hotel curve on to the Caley Promenade at Rhos-on-Sea. The old Rhos pier can be seen to the left of the view. Judging by the trees and the 'white tops' out to sea, there must have been a strong wind blowing on this September day in 1953. *H. B. Priestley, NTM*

Below left Another tram jam! On this occasion, 9 August 1948, it is a result of 'close poling'; that is to say that somewhere along the route a two-trolley tram has got too close to one of the open-top double-deck cars and its leading trolley has touched the top deck mesh (which was earthed) and shorted out the supply of electrical current. Three trams are held up here on the Promenade at Rhos-on-Sea. (Did anybody think to bring sandwiches?) Note the variety of cast-iron street furniture on the Promenade. *H. B. Priestley, NTM*

Above right One of the streamlined double-deck trams, No 24, is operating on the Colwyn Bay-Rhos-on-Sea local service, which ran as far as the tram depot on Penrhyn Avenue. The group of visitors on the benches to the right are well wrapped up - not the warmest of days in June 1948, a year that is otherwise recalled for its particularly warm summer. Rhos pier, in the background, was opened in 1896 and was privately owned for most of its life. It became derelict in the early 1950s, and Colwyn Bay Council bought it in 1953 with a view to improving the pier and the general appearance of the area as a whole. Ultimately it was decided not to repair it, and the 1,240-foot-long structure was blown up instead, with the buildings around the entrance being generally tidied up and refurbished. *Photographer unknown*

Below The long straight of Penrhyn Avenue is seen from the top deck of a Colwyn Bay-bound tram. On the westbound track, ex-Accrington No 4 has just pulled away from the Request stop outside the cricket ground, and a motorist is manoeuvring to accelerate past it. The poster in the extreme bottom left is advertising the famous 'star-maker' Carroll Levis, who would be appearing at the Arcadia in Colwyn Bay. Levis had a very popular radio talent show in the 1950s called *Carroll Levis and his Discoveries*. Years later, Hughie Green would compere an even more successful show on television - *Opportunity Knocks*. *H. B. Priestley, NTM*

Above This undated view was taken on the top deck of a Llandudno-bound tram at the Church Road stop by the tram depot on Penrhyn Avenue. Fashions include a navy blue gabardine school mackintosh with hood and the newer lightweight plastic 'packamack', which could be wrapped up and carried in your pocket, yet kept you reasonably dry in a light shower of rain. The two-and-one seating arrangement can be seen, as well as the wet-and-dry-weather boards on the seats; if the seats were wet, a hinged board could be tipped over to provide a dry seat to sit on.

When the passenger stood up the board, which was counter-balanced, reverted to its original position. *A. D. Packer*

Below Ex-Bournemouth trams pass at the Church Road stop on the morning of 26 August 1955. The trio on the left appear to be ready for a day on the beach, while the dog appears pleased to be off the tram and is obviously enjoying a brief lie down without any vibration under his paws. *H. B. Priestley, NTM*

This photograph was taken by the late Maurice O'Connor outside the tram depot on 1 June 1955. A double-deck tram has been brought into service to replace No 5, which has developed a fault. Passengers can be seen alighting and transferring to the tram in front while No 11 approaches from Penrhyn Bay. The wind has caught the skirt of the lady to the left of the tram, giving the impression that she is wearing a pair of striped bloomers! *M. J. O'Connor, NTM*

Ex-Bournemouth tram No 11 clears track works on Penrhyn Avenue and accelerates towards Orme Point. The roadway was opened up to repack and replace sleepers during July 1949. The only warning to motorists that can be seen are two red flags mounted on iron poles at the far end of the roadworks. *H. B. Priestley, NTM*

Above When Ministry of Transport approval was given to operate the streamlined double-deck trams Nos 23 and 24, it was stipulated that no passengers should travel on them between Rhos-on-Sea and Llandudno over Penrhyn Hill. No 23 is seen here making its way along Marine Drive in Penrhyn Bay to take up local service in Llandudno on 6 August 1948. The supply of current to the overhead wires can be seen just beyond the tram. From this point back to Colwyn Bay the electricity had been provided by Colwyn Bay power station since 1932. The county boundary between Denbighshire (Clwyd) and Caernarvonshire (Gwynedd) was situated about 50 yards beyond the tram. *H. B. Priestley, NTM*

Below Driver Reg Johnson takes a brief opportunity to sit down and have a word with conductor Jock Nicholson while they wait for No 8 to clear the single-line section. By May 1955, the date of this view, work was already well advanced on the new sea wall and promenade, and contractors' vehicles and plant are much in evidence. *Eric Thornton*

Left Bill Roberts takes ex-Bournemouth tram No 8 into the single-line section on Marine Drive on 19 August 1953, with a toast-rack working an 'extra' duty behind him. *H. B. Priestley, NTM*

Below left Looking towards Glan-y-Mor Road, the effects of the sea can be seen. As toast-rack No 19 moves slowly past a genera-tor, a group of people stand by the temporary fence looking down at the devastation. The replacement bracket arms have been erected, making redundant the other poles, which carried span wires. The photograph was taken on 16 August 1954, and scaf-folding still remains by a pair of new houses that are being adver-tised for sale. *H. B. Priestley, NTM*

Above Viewed from the opposite direction on 6 June 1954, the problem looks even worse. Tram No 8 is on a private tour of the line, and time has been taken for the members of the Light Railway Transport League to alight and get a closer look. Chief inspector Ernie Woolley keeps an eye on things while photographers try to get the best angle for their photographs. *R. J. S. Wiseman*

Right On 28 July 1948 an unidentified toast-rack climbs up from Penrhyn Bay into Glan-y-Mor Road. The terraced properties on the right are known as Quarry Cottages and were originally built to accommodate workers at the nearby quarry on the Little Orme. Also visible but not in regular use are the facing points that enabled trams to work single line as far as the Golf House in an emergency. *H. B. Priestley, NTM*

Above By 1955, when this picture was taken, the remaining plots of land on the left along Glan-y-Mor Road had been sold and the houses extended up to the top of the road near St David's Corner. The state of the private road at least ensured that no unwanted traffic passed along it! *A. D. Packer*

Below The tramway at St David's Corner, the junction of Penrhyn Isaf Road and Glan-y-Mor Road, had a distinctly 'interurban' look and feel about it, probably due to the unmade road. There are several people in evidence including the four passengers who alighted from the tram. A delivery van in the background has pulled well over to the left to avoid blocking the tram track. *A. D. Packer*

Opposite page Ex-Accrington tram No 1 pauses briefly to take a passenger on board at the Little Orme Cafe stop before climbing the 1 in 11 Penrhyn Hill. One of the tram company's wooden shelters can be seen. The picture was taken just after the war, but before the tram shelters had their nameboards fitted.

In 1996 the new dual carriageway on Penrhyn Hill can be seen, the former trackbed having been widened in 1971 to accommodate the new roadway. *D. W. K Jones, NTM/Stuart A. Rivers*

Above The angle of this photograph gives the scene a truly rural view, the busy Llandudno Road lying out of sight below the tram to the left. Power feeder cables are in evidence on the bracket arm under which the tram is about to pass. Tram drivers on the uphill climb would have to shut off their controller handle quickly, then notch it back up again to avoid losing speed. Failure to follow this procedure would result in a big electric arc flashing across the insulated part of the section breaker fitted into the overhead wire as the trolley wheel passed under it.

For the tram driving test, new men would be examined by a senior Inspector. Using a normal service tram with passengers on board, the Inspector would cut the power off while the tram was climbing the hill to see if the driver reacted quickly and correctly. On one occasion a new driver, when asked what procedure he would adopt if the power failed while climbing the hill, replied that he would apply the electric brake.

'But you have got no power,' replied the examiner.

'Then I would apply the hand brake,' said the novice.

'Linkage has just snapped and the tram has started to run backwards,' retorted the examiner.

'Oh dear - well, in that case I would run to the other end and change the destination to "Colwyn Bay"!' *H. B. Priestley, NTM*

Above right Streamlined tram No 24 is pictured climbing Penrhyn Hill on its way to take up the local service in Llandudno. On one such occasion the driver of a Crosville bus that was climbing up the hill adjacent to the tramway was amazed when one of these cars overtook him with consummate ease, giving him the impression that his own vehicle had stopped. He was used to either being ahead of the trams on this stretch, or at least keeping up with them. The tram driver had obviously driven up the hill in 'full parallel', contrary to regulations, but it ably demonstrated the power that these trams had. *Photographer unknown*

Right The tram track towards Llandudno passed close to the rock face on Bryn-y-Bia Road, so conductors on the toast-racks travelling in that direction were forbidden to collect fares from the running boards until the tram was well clear of this section. One conductor chose to ignore the rule and was lucky to escape with bad scuff marks to the heels of his shoes! The courting couple on the top deck of this tram seem to be enjoying the relative solitude of their journey. *A. D. Packer*

This superb view, taken here on 27 August 1953, greeted passengers when their tram left Bryn-y-Bia Road and entered the Bodafon Fields. The full panorama on a clear day would include Anglesey and Puffin Island as well as Penmaenmawr mountain, Llandudno with both its bays, and of course the Great Orme. Today, 'Ty Mostyn', a detached residence, stands on the spot where No 6 is shown. Bryn-y-Bia Road falls away to the right while Bodafon Road, a narrow, winding lane to the left, leads along the hillside towards Craig-y-Don. *H. B. Priestley, NTM*

Above Rivalry always existed between the trams and Crosville, and it was not always friendly. Here the race is on for passengers in Craig-y-Don, with a new Bristol Lodekka bus chasing after tram No 2 down Bryn-y-Bia Road. The tram route was the more direct down through the Bodafon Fields to Nant-y-Gamar Road; the bus had to take a detour out to the Promenade and along to Queens Road, where it would try to get in front of the tram and pick up the majority of passengers who would be waiting there. Sometimes the bus would win, sometimes the tram would just have the edge. As far as the tram crews were concerned, it depended on whether they would have to stop at Nant-y-Gamar and Carmen Sylva Roads. If so the race was probably lost unless, during the summer, the bus was slowed down in traffic on the Promenade. Great fun! *A. D. Packer*

Below Toast-rack No 21 negotiates the Craigside curve on its descent towards Llandudno. At night, when competing for passengers at Craig-y-Don, some tram crews were adept at letting the tram coast down the hill at quite a fast speed with the trolley pulled down off the overhead wire so that no lights would be visible. Crews on the chasing Crosville buses could then not see where the tram was, and eased up along the Promenade only to find that the tram had beaten them to Craig-y-Don when they saw its lights go on as it approached Nant-y-Gamar Road. *H. B. Priestley, NTM*

Above A passenger's eye view from the from seat of a toast-rack as it heads towards Craig-y-Don, with ex-Bournemouth car No 7 approaching with a good load bound for Colwyn Bay. The twin wires mounted on the traction poles on the right-hand side carried the electric current along the route to the various distribution boxes located at regular intervals (usually every half-mile), where the supply was fed into the overhead wires. *M. J. O'Connor, NTM*

Below Seen from the top deck of No 15 as the Nant-y-Gamar Road stop is reached, No 14 has just entered the fields on her journey eastwards. Four passengers are waiting to board our tram, which is just about to clatter through the crossover used by the Llandudno 'local' cars. The small bird perched on the trolley wire would fly off before the tram's trolley-wheel could clip its claws! *M. J. O'Connor, NTM*

With a rumble, No 15 leaves Bodafon Fields and rejoins the street track in Mostyn Avenue on 29 August 1953. Despite the damp day, passengers have not been deterred from riding on the top deck. *R. B. Parr, NTM*

Above Passengers board No 6 on Mostyn Avenue at its junction with Carmen Sylva Road, the latter named after the visit of Queen Elisabeth of Roumania in 1890. When she left the town after a five-week holiday she described Wales as 'a beautiful haven of peace'. Her words were ultimately translated for Llandudno's town motto, which is 'Hardd, Hafan, Hedd'. *A. D. Packer*

Below Looking towards Llandudno from the tram stop at Queens Road on Mostyn Avenue, a solitary passenger steps out into the road to board No 6, which approaches from town. Bicycles, delivery vans and a handcart are all in evidence in this 1954 view. *H. B. Priestley, NTM*

Above It is late afternoon on 26 August 1955 and ex-Bournemouth tram No 11 leaves Craig-y-Don for Llandudno. St Paul's Church, Mostyn Broadway, is in the background and the field to the left is part of a large 'Pitch and Putt' green that extended back from the Broadway to the Promenade. *H. B. Priestley, NTM*

Below A view taken from the front seat of a toast-rack tram looking along Mostyn Broadway as tram No 6 approaches, heading for Colwyn Bay. The poor road surface occupied by the tramway is much in evidence; little wonder that Llandudno Council was continually pressing the company to rectify the matter. The land to the left contained allotments, which, for those keen gardeners who planted rhubarb, produced bumper crops, due no doubt to the marshy sub-soil. This foundation was in all probability a major contributory factor to the poor state of the road surface generally along Mostyn Broadway. *R. B. Parr, NTM*

Below On an overcast day in August 1954 ex-Bournemouth tram No 13 pulls away from the North Western Hotel towards the centre of Llandudno, while Crosville buses jostle for position in the background. The double-deck bus is a Leyland PD1A dating from 1947 (GFM 908, fleet No M523) operating on the 455 service via St Asaph and Colwyn Bay. The Ford van was new in 1953. On the opposite corner, the Lunt sisters' millinery shop occupies a prominent position in the building belonging to the Broadway Hotel. *R. B. Parr, NTM*

Bottom A lovely view looking along Mostyn Street in August 1951, taken from the rear of a toast-rack tram outside the library as it waits to enter the single-line section. The column supporting the tram's trolley pole, together with its passenger lights and notice, can easily be seen. Holidaymakers pack the pavements and quite a variety of vehicles are parked on the left-hand side of the road.

Parking on Mostyn Street alternated from one side to the other depending on whether it was an 'odd' or 'even' day of the month. Circular iron plates fitted with hinged flaps and mounted on top of columns advised motorists accordingly. A lady's bicycle is also to be seen parked on the kerb edge on the right. *H. B. Priestley, NTM*

Right An Austin Ruby is parked close to the zebra crossing at the end of Mostyn Street and pedestrians pause and chat as ex-Bournemouth tram No 12 arrives with a full complement of passengers and prepares to negotiate the tight curve leading into the loop at the corner of Gloddaeth Street. One of the notices advising of the parking restrictions mentioned opposite can also be seen. *A. D. Packer*

Below right At about 9 am on 9 August 1949 ex-Accrington tram No 3 arrives at Palladium Corner just as ex-Bournemouth tram No 10 waits to enter Mostyn Street. An Inspector prepares to alight from the tram when it reaches its stop, to commence his duties for the day regulating the trams at this busy location. The Crosville bus seen on the left, new that year, was part of a batch built by Leyland for Cumberland Motor Services. The last eight vehicles of that order were diverted to Crosville, but not before they had received their Cumberland registration numbers. Between the tram and the bus, early shoppers are about and the shopkeepers on the corner of Upper Mostyn Street have got their sun-blinds down in readiness for another hot day.

The points in the track in the foreground were acquired from Birkenhead in 1937. In 1996 North West Water opened up the centre of Mostyn Street to replace a large sewer drain, and in the process much of the former tram track was removed. The points seen in the picture were presented to the Llandudno Museum on Gloddaeth Street and can be seen in the front garden there. *H. B. Priestley, NTM*

This page Another early morning view looking along Gloddaeth Street and showing Palladium Corner. Two trams pause on the passing loop while intending passengers approach the open-top double-deck tram. The ornate facade of the Palladium cinema behind the single-deck tram is plainly visible, while to the extreme right the larger Odeon cinema building can be made out, with scaffolding erected for repairs.

By 1996 some of the shops have changed and both the Palladium cinema, built in 1920, and the English Presbyterian Church are still in evidence. The Odeon has been demolished and replaced with a modern housing development. *Eric Thornton/author*

Right A Ford Zephyr four-door saloon is parked nearest the camera in a picture that shows the car parking arrangements along Gloddaeth Street. The ornate tower of the English Presbyterian Church is seen on the right as ex-Accrington tram No 3 heads towards West Shore on 13 May 1955. *A. D. Packer*

Below right Tram No 3 is seen near the Oval on Gloddaeth Avenue making good speed towards West Shore. The advertisement board on its roof features 'Clare's for Fashions', Llandudno's oldest and (then) largest department store. Observe the wide thoroughfare that was originally laid out in the early 1900s before the arrival of the tramway. Note also the gas lamp with its extended column. The bar sticking out from its side was for maintenance men to lean their ladders against, which enabled them to climb up and gain access to the lamp. *R. B. Parr, NTM*

Journey's end! Ex-Bournemouth tram No 8, having arrived from Colwyn Bay, has its trolley turned as passengers alight from both decks. It will be appreciated that the conductor had to be careful when turning the trolley in case he banged someone on the head with it! As soon as this task is completed the tram will depart immediately, trying, particularly in the summer months, to keep on time. Generally between 40 and 43 minutes was allowed for the journey in each direction during the summer, but traffic conditions often disrupted the timetable. Right at the end of the line a gentleman in a motorised invalid carriage takes a rest and enjoys the sunshine and the passing scene at West Shore on 22 August 1954. *H. B. Priestley, NTM*

THE LAST DAY

ON SATURDAY 24 MARCH 1956 this unique tramway closed down. A combination of factors had eventually forced the issue, not the least of which was old age and poverty. A private take-over to keep the trams running and re-develop their tourist potential had been scuppered in favour of the acquisition of a fleet of near-life-expired second-hand utility buses, which had been built variously between 1938 and 1946. Even casual observers felt that the 'Red' buses would not last very long.

On the last day of tram operation scores of people travelled from different parts of the country for a last ride and to say their own private goodbyes to an old friend. The following photographs serve to illustrate some of the highlights of that day.

Author

Even the welding gear made an appearance! There was a problem with the worn track at Brompton Avenue, where the track turned sharply on to the railway bridge, which had caused a minor derailment early in the morning. The breakdown crew were on the scene fairly quickly and effected a temporary repair - after all, it only had to last another 15 hours! Fred Ward was on hand to photograph Tom Evans welding the offending spot. The bamboo pole with cable attached was hooked on to the overhead wire to obtain current for the generator. *F. E. J. Ward*

Above In Llandudno on board No 14, a well-wrapped-up conductress, Doris Sprout, collects the fares from an equally well-wrapped-up group of passengers. Being an organised conductress, Doris had collected all the fares before the tram moved off. A lot of the tickets issued on the last day would be ninepenny through tickets, certainly far more than usual for the time of the year! *A. D. Packer*

Below It's now late morning, and No 14 picks up a few locals at the Nant-y-Gamar Road stop. The gentleman on the step looks as if he is waiting for the photographer as conductor Michael (Mickey) Morris looks on. A little over five years later, although he did not know it at the time, Morris would drive the last company-owned 'Red' bus off the road in May 1961. *A. D. Packer*

No 11 stops for passengers at Queens Road, Craig-y-Don. Someone makes a point of having a word with the tram driver, perhaps to wish him luck. Although the morning was bright, the sun had not broken through the mist and this picture captures that atmosphere very well indeed. To the right a Triumph Renown (sometimes known as a 'Razor-Edge' Triumph) turns towards town. *A. D. Packer*

Above During the morning a group of former tram drivers from Bournemouth travelled up overnight to be able to have one last drive of the trams on which they used to work until 1936. No 8 was put at their disposal and, with Chief Inspector Ernie Woolley keeping an eye on things, the men took it in turns to drive the tram over the full length of the line. Here No 8 is about to go into the depot after their 'tour', but they have had to wait until No 11 passes before they can use the crossover. A depot fitter waits to put the trolley on the opposite wire, while Conductor Bob Morgan can be seen on the rear platform of No 11. The Bournemouth party were treated to a buffet in the canteen by their hosts before they returned to the South Coast. *A. D. Packer*

Below The mist had still not lifted by early afternoon as 'Farmer' Dick Hughes brought No 14 up towards Craigside with a group of enthusiasts on the top deck, including the author seated next to the top deck light. *A. D. Packer*

Above Mid-afternoon at the Maesgwyn Road stop, No 11 damaged her lifeguard tray and had to be coaxed to the depot. Although the breakdown gang could remove part of the problem, something still dragged along the ground making an awful noise. By the time No 11 was capable of being moved, No 4 had caught up with her. *R. J. S. Wiseman*

Below On arrival at the depot, No 11 was shunted out of service and was replaced by No 13. A small group of onlookers watch the scene as No 13 is brought out on to Penrhyn Avenue. One of the replacement 'Red' buses is visible, together with the new fuel storage tank that had been erected over the entrance to road 5. *A. D. Packer*

Left Determined to make the most of the sun that broke through the mist during the late afternoon, photographers try to get a good shot of No 4, which was about to pass them in the Bodafon Fields. *J. W. Martin, courtesy of Brian P. Martin*

Middle left A little after 10 pm, 'Farmer' Dick Hughes and his conductor, Bob Morgan, bring No 8 through from the depot to the North Western Hotel to await the official party, who are gathered at a function to commemorate the event in the nearby Imperial Hotel. The tram is pictured here just after its arrival at the end of Mostyn Broadway. *Graphic Studios, Llandudno*

Bottom left The invitation to the Imperial Hotel. *Author's collection*

The Chairman and Directors of

Llandudno & Colwyn Bay Electric Railway Ltd.

request the pleasure of the company of

_____

at the Imperial Hotel, Llandudno

on Saturday, 24ᵗʰ March 1956.

R.S.V.P. The Secretary,
Suffolk House,
Cocktails 9.00-10.00 p.m.   *Laurence Pountney Hill.*
Dress informal   *London. E.C.4*

THE LAST TRAM WILL LEAVE THE NORTH WESTERN HOTEL FOR WEST SHORE TO COLWYN BAY AT 10.15 P.M.

Above right The last public service tramcar to leave West Shore was No 4, one of the ex-Accrington trams. Driven by Percy Larkman, its departure was delayed due to a controller fault. A crowd of well-wishers from the West Shore district has gathered to witness the event. *A. D. Packer*

Right By the time No 4 reached the depot her controller problem had got worse and she had been running so slowly that the Last Tram caught up with her. She was replaced by No 3, which had already reached the depot on her last trip. Seat cushions had to be hastily found as all those inside No 3 had been had been removed for souvenirs. The photograph shows the transfer of passengers and seats taking place! *F. E. J. Ward*

Above Eventually No 8 crested the hill in Abergele Road and rolled down towards the terminus, Chief Inspector Ernie Woolley bringing her to the end of the line for the last time. Some 25 years earlier he had brought the last tram down from Old Colwyn to the same spot but from the opposite direction. Press Photographer Jim Parry of Rhyl was responsible for this excellent photograph, which shows some of the large crowd who had gathered around to see the event, even though the hour was late. The tram departed just after midnight, accompanied by cheering and singing and a cavalcade of cars and motorcycles that followed it back to the depot. *Jim Parry*

Below At approximately 12.15 am on Sunday morning, 25 March 1956, No 8 arrives back at the depot. Seen alighting are Walter Butterworth and, next to him, Stanley Dudman, Director and Secretary of the company. The dog, taken out for its late evening walk, was probably unused to seeing so much activity at that time of night. The tram was driven off the road into the depot yard by Ernie Woolley. Another chapter in the life of the company had drawn to a close. *A. D. Packer*

Above The second-hand buses that replaced the trams were not the answer to the company's problem. Over the five years they were operated, there were continual differences of opinion between the company and Crosville regarding timetables and the thorny question of duplication during the summer months. The drivers of the 'Red' buses tried their hardest to ensure that they got to the bus stops first, particularly to the busiest ones, and tempers often became frayed. In fact, the situation could quite easily be compared to the immediate de-regulation days of the mid-1980s. Crosville was in a position to flood the area with its newest buses, and generally did. A ride in one of their open-top buses was far more comfortable than the top deck of a 'Red' bus, which still had wooden seats. An added factor in the general decline of passengers was the increase in private car ownership. This photograph at West Shore in 1957 shows one of the opposition's relatively new open-top buses with two 'Red' vehicles, Nos 9 and 3 (1), both ex-Southdown Guy Arab 5LWs with Weymann and Northern Counties bodywork respectively, dating from 1945. *K. W. Swallow*

Below The debate over road-reinstatement came to a head after the tram company pulled up its track in Penrhyn Avenue and left compressed ballast and grit in its place; buses travelling towards Colwyn Bay used what bit of tarmac surface remained. When operating towards Llandudno, the buses operated along Abbey Road, which ran parallel to Penrhyn Avenue. Here 'Red' bus No 12 makes its way towards Rhos-on-Sea. The now redundant tram poles with their truncated bracket arms await removal. *K. W. Swallow*

The notices advising motorists of the toll road were in situ until the road was bought by the local authority. It is understood that these particular boards were given to an enthusiast following his approaches to Colwyn Bay Council. I wonder if they still exist? In the background bus No 7 heads towards Llandudno, while in the immediate foreground remains of the tram track here at Orme Point can still be seen. *K. W. Swallow*

THE RE-INTRODUCTION of the steamer service between Liverpool, Llandudno and Menai Bridge in 1946 was another sign that things were beginning to get back to normal after five long years of wartime restrictions. TSS *St Seriol* got a big welcome when she arrived at Llandudno Pier on Good Friday, 25 April 1946. She was soon re-joined by her sister ships, TSS *St Tudno* and the smaller TSMV *St Trillo*. The latter vessel had carried the name *St Silio* from her launch in 1936, but in 1945 a decision was taken by her owners, the Liverpool & North Wales Steamship Co Ltd, to re-name her. The yellow funnels of this fleet were most distinctive (*St Trillo* had two) and considerable interest was aroused whenever a steamer approached the pier.

Popular excursions during the period up to 1961 were from Llandudno to Anglesey (*St Trillo*), Llandudno to Douglas (*St Seriol*) and Llandudno to Menai Bridge; the latter was usually performed by *St Tudno* as an extension of its daily trip from Liverpool.

In January 1962 *St Seriol* was laid up in Birkenhead as an economy measure. By March she had been put up for sale and was subsequently towed to Holland for scrap. *St Tudno* fulfilled all the sailings from Liverpool, working every day throughout the season. Her final voyage to North Wales was on 27 August 1962, after which she too was eventually sold and scrapped. The following year the route was taken over by ships of the Isle of Man Steam Packet Co Ltd. *St Trillo* continued to operate the sailing from Llandudno to Menai Bridge under ownership of P. & A. Campbell in their White Funnel fleet. She was withdrawn from duties in North Wales *circa* 1970.

Both illustrations author's collection

SAILINGS FROM LLANDUDNO

(Weather and other circumstances permitting)
Subject to alteration without notice

s.s. St. Tudno ★ s.s. St. Seiriol ★ m.v. St. Trillo

EVERY DAY (Sundays included)

UNTIL MONDAY, 20th SEPTEMBER

		Single	Day Excursion
1-15 p.m. ST. TUDNO or ST. SEIRIOL	**MENAI BRIDGE** (1 Hour Ashore) Through picturesque Menai Strait. Due 2-40 p.m. Return, 3-45 p.m. Due Llandudno, 5-0 p.m.	4/6	6/-
Sundays excepted	**CIRCULAR TOUR** Out by boat, return by any Crosville bus	—	6/9 Children 3/9
Sundays included	Out by boat, return by rail (any train)	—	7/6
5-15 p.m. ST. TUDNO or ST. SEIRIOL	**LIVERPOOL** Due 7-40 p.m.	8/6	Period 15/-

SUNDAYS

		Single	Day Excursion
10-45 a.m. ST. TRILLO	**MORNING CRUISE** Viewing the Great Orme and Puffin Island. Due back, 12-30 p.m.	—	3/-
2-45 p.m. ST. TRILLO	**AFTERNOON CRUISE** To Puffin Island and towards Red Wharf Bay. Due back, 4-45 p.m.	—	4/-
7-30 p.m. ST. TRILLO	**GRAND EVENING CRUISE** Towards Puffin Island. Due back, 9-0 p.m.	—	3/-

MONDAYS

		Single	Day Excursion
10-45 a.m. ST. TRILLO	**MORNING CRUISE** Viewing the Great Orme and Puffin Island. Due back, 12-30 p.m.	—	3/-
2-30 p.m. ST. TRILLO	**MENAI BRIDGE** To see the famous Suspension Bridge. Due, 4-0 p.m. Return, 4-30 p.m. Due Llandudno, 6-0 p.m.	4/6	6/-
7-30 p.m. ST. TRILLO	**EVENING CRUISE** Towards Puffin Island. Due back, 9-0 p.m.	—	3/-

TUESDAYS

		Single	Day Excursion
10-15 a.m. ST. SEIRIOL (until 7th Sept.)	**DOUGLAS** (Isle of Man) Due, 1-40 p.m. Return, 4-30 p.m. About three hours ashore—due back, 8-0 p.m. Bus tour from Peveril Square. Tickets from the Purser, 1/6.	10/-	15/-
10-45 a.m. ST. TRILLO	**MENAI BRIDGE** (Isle of Anglesey) 3½ hours ashore to visit beauty spots. St. Trillo St. Tudno Return 12-45 p.m. 3-45 p.m. Due Llandudno 2-15 p.m. 5-0 p.m.	4/6	6/-
2-45 p.m. ST. TRILLO	**AFTERNOON CRUISE** To Puffin Island and towards Red Wharf Bay. Due back, 4-45 p.m.	—	4/-
6-45 p.m. ST. TRILLO	**EVENING CIRCULAR TOUR** Through Menai Strait to Menai Bridge. Due, 8-15 p.m. Return by Crosville bus, Post Office Square, 8-30, 8-47 p.m. Due Llandudno, 10-20, 10-40 p.m.	4/6	5/9 Children 3/3

WEDNESDAYS

		Single	Day Excursion
10-15 a.m. ST. SEIRIOL (until 8th Sept.)	**DOUGLAS** (Isle of Man) Due, 1-40 p.m. Return, 4-30 p.m. About three hours ashore—due back, 8-0 p.m. Bus tour from Peveril Square. Tickets from the Purser, 1/6.	10/-	15/-
10-45 a.m. ST. TRILLO	**MORNING CRUISE** Viewing the Great Orme and Puffin Island. Due back, 12-30 p.m.	—	3/-
2-30 p.m. ST. TRILLO	**MENAI BRIDGE** Grand mountain and marine scenery. Due, 4-0 p.m. Return, 4-30 p.m. Due Llandudno, 6-0 p.m.	4/6	6/-
7-30 p.m. ST. TRILLO	**GRAND EVENING CRUISE** Towards Puffin Island. Due back, 9-0 p.m.	—	3/-

THURSDAYS

		Single	Day Excursion
(Commencing 8th July) 9-30 a.m. ST. SEIRIOL (until 9th Sept.)	**LIVERPOOL** (Two hours ashore) Due, 12-0 noon. Return from Liverpool, 2-0 p.m. Due Llandudno, 4-30 p.m.	—	7/-
10-45 a.m. ST. TRILLO	**MENAI BRIDGE** (Isle of Anglesey) 3½ hours ashore to visit beauty spots. St. Trillo St. Tudno Return 12-45 p.m. 3-45 p.m. Due Llandudno 2-15 p.m. 5-0 p.m.	4/6	6/-
2-45 p.m. ST. TRILLO	**AFTERNOON CRUISE** To Puffin Island and towards Red Wharf Bay. Due back, 4-45 p.m.	—	4/-
6-45 p.m. ST. TRILLO	**EVENING CIRCULAR TOUR** Through Menai Strait to Menai Bridge. Due, 8-15 p.m. Return by Crosville bus, Post Office Square, 8-30, 8-47 p.m. Due Llandudno, 10-20, 10-40 p.m.	4/6	5/9 Children 3/3

FRIDAYS

		Single	Day Excursion
10-45 a.m. ST. TRILLO	**MORNING CRUISE** Viewing the Great Orme and Puffin Island. Due back, 12-30 p.m.	—	3/-
2-30 p.m. ST. TRILLO	**MENAI BRIDGE** A delightful cruise through Menai Strait. Due, 4-0 p.m. Return 4-30 p.m. Due Llandudno, 6-0 p.m.	4/6	6/-
6-45 p.m. ST. TRILLO	**EVENING CIRCULAR TOUR** Through Menai Strait to Menai Bridge. Due, 8-15 p.m. Return by Crosville bus, Post Office Square, 8-30, 8-47 p.m. Due Llandudno, 10-20, 10-40 p.m.	4/6	5/9 Children 3/3

All tickets are issued, passengers and goods carried subject to the Company's conditions of carriage as exhibited at the Company's offices and on the vessels.
Children over 3 and under 14 years, half fare.
Buffets and refreshment bars on all vessels. Lunches and teas served on St. Tudno and St. Seiriol only.
Weekly Season Tickets (not transferable and not available Sundays) 20/- (pier tolls excluded) issued from any date and available all advertised sailings of the Company's vessels from Llandudno. Not available on bus circular tours.
Official Guide obtainable at Company's office, pier gates or on board vessels, price 6d.
Through rail bookings in connection with the above sailings are in operation from Prestatyn, Rhyl, Abergele, Old Colwyn, Colwyn Bay, Llandudno Junction, Llanfairfechan, Penmaenmawr and Bangor.

A lovely picture of *St Tudno* arriving at Llandudno Pier on the morning sailing from Liverpool. Passengers could alight here and spend a few hours ashore before gathering on the pier for the late afternoon return to Liverpool. Other passengers would remain on the vessel, to be joined by holidaymakers from Llandudno for the sail around the Great Orme to Menai Bridge and back. The ship is packed with day-trippers, and people on the pier have gathered to see its arrival. Sundresses, sports jackets, summer hats, even the odd pair of braces, all combine to create this delightful holiday scene - and not a pair of denims or trainers in sight. Great! *Stuart Bale Ltd, Liverpool*

St Seriol going full astern from Llandudno Pier. *Photographer unknown*

St Trillo at Llandudno, with *St Seriol* in the background. *Photographer unknown*

=THE GREAT ORME RAILWAY=

THE GREAT ORME TRAMWAY was opened in 1902. Roads had existed on the slopes of the Orme, but due to their steepness they were difficult to negotiate and the people who lived on the lower slopes had to walk down into the town, then walk back up to their houses carrying their provisions. As Llandudno became a popular holiday resort, the idea of a cable-hauled tramway up the mountain was developed, and the line as we know it today has benefited holidaymakers and residents alike.

The line is divided into two sections, lower and upper, both controlled from a winding house situated on a plateau known as Halfway Station. On the lower section the cables hauling the trams are contained in a slot between the running rails. As one tram is hauled up, the other is lowered, and they pass at a loop midway between Victoria Station in Church Walks and Halfway Station. From the mid-point loop, the trams run on interlaced track to ensure that their cables do not come in contact with each other. Communication between trams and winding house was originally by telephone, the trolleys making the contact with the overhead wire.

At its steepest point the gradient of the lower section is about 1 in 4, and as a consequence the cars on this section are hauled with heavier cables than those on the upper section and they are also equipped with additional brakes that come into immediate effect if the cable should go slack during operation. These are rigorously tested before the start of each season.

The upper section to the summit is also cable-hauled, the cables running exposed between the rails over a series of rollers and pulleys. The winding gear was originally steam driven but was replaced by electricity during the winter of 1957/58. The original trams, built by Hurst Nelson & Co Ltd of Motherwell, Nos 4, 5, 6 and 7, are still in operation. Three four-wheel vans with platforms, Nos 1-3, were used for testing purposes before the line was opened. Subsequently they carried equipment and materials up the line, usually being propelled in front of an empty passenger car. These vehicles had disappeared by 1930.

The tramway was in private ownership until 1948, when Llandudno Urban District Council exercised its option to buy it, taking over on 1 January 1949. Today the line is as popular as ever. The method of operation has been streamlined and the communication between trams and control is by personal two-way radios, which have replaced the more familiar trolleys. The word 'Tramway' has also been re-instated on the side of the trams.

A selection of Great Orme Railway tickets. *Author's collection*

Author's collection

1924.

The
Great Orme Tramways
Company.

Statement of Accounts

JANUARY 1st to DECEMBER 31st,
1924.

NOTICE IS HEREBY GIVEN that the Annual Meeting of the Shareholders of the above Company will be held at Midland Bank Chambers, 46, Mostyn Street, Llandudno, on Wednesday, the 11th day of February, 1925, at 3 o'clock p.m., for the election of Directors, the election of Auditor, and for the transaction of the General Business of the Company.

Dated this 28th day of January, 1925.

JOHN OWEN, *Chairman.*
HENRY SUTCLIFFE,
Secretary and Manager.

Victoria Station,
Church Walks,
Llandudno.

"Advertiser" Printing Works, Llandudno.

Cars 6 and 7 are about to pass each other at the midway point of the upper section. The points are tripped by the trams passing over them so they will always follow the path of their respective cables. In the middle distance can be seen the winding house and depot buildings, while the site on the right, beyond the motor cars, has since been developed as the Great Orme Copper Mines. The trams today wear a livery that is best described as an unfortunate by-product of the 1990s, but with the centenary of the line only a few years away, it is to be hoped that they will assume a livery more in keeping with their Victorian heritage. *English Electric Co Ltd*

Above Victoria Station was a familiar landmark on Church Walks, forming lower terminal of the Great Orme tramway. This *circa* 1958 scene (dated by the films on offer at the Odeon) shows a variety of penny-in-the-slot machines in front of the station railings (there was even one for self-inducing an electric shock!) together with various advertisements for cinemas, theatres and excursions. A trip to York and back for 20 shillings (£1) is being offered by British Railways. Another attraction on the Orme was the Alice in Wonderland Garden in the Happy Valley. Although the basic station structure still stands today, the site underwent considerable improvement in the latter part of the 1980s, making an altogether more attractive approach to the line. *Photographer unknown*

Left An unusual scene taken during a winter maintenance programme. Workmen are using the roof of tram No 5 to attend to the overhead wire near St Beuno's Road on the approach to Halfway Station. Part of Llandudno is visible in the middle distance. *John L. Reay, courtesy of Stuart A. Rivers*

RHYL MINIATURE TRAMWAY

ANOTHER TRAMWAY that nearly operated in Colwyn Bay was created by Claude Lane, whose business was the manufacture of light electric road vehicles. Claude was a tram enthusiast, and in 1948 he built a replica model tram based on the streamlined cars that were then operating on the Llandudno & Colwyn Bay Electric Railway. The tram could carry 23 small children on two decks, and was paraded around local garden fetes in Barnet, Hitchin and Uxbridge running on 15-inch-gauge portable track and powered by a generator.

It was Claude's intention to find a permanent site for the tram, and it appeared in St Leonards, near Hastings, during the summer of 1951. However, meeting with opposition, the tramway was dismantled and different

venues were approached, including Colwyn Bay and Rhyl. Colwyn Bay Council discussed the request on 3 April 1952; the suggestion was that the tram would occupy a site at the foot of the railway embankment on the promenade wall. The Council at this time was having problems with the L&CBER, and the thought of more trams did not appeal, so it resolved to take no further action.

Rhyl, on the other hand, was quick to spot an attraction and gave permission for a line to be laid in the Vroyd Amusement Park at the west end of the Promenade. As built it consisted of a single line about a quarter of a mile long and included a double

Denis Butler

Trams 6 and 23 are pictured together at the West Parade terminus of the narrow-gauge tramline that operated in the Vroyd Amusement Park at Rhyl between 1952 and 1957. Judging by the state of the weather, business was slow that day! *Brian Martin, courtesy of Denis Butler*

track stub at each end and a two-road tram shed. Power to the overhead wire at 60 volts DC was provided by a transformer rectifier and traction batteries. The line opened at Whitsuntide 1952. A second tram, an open 'boat' based on the vehicles running in Blackpool, had been built and, numbered 225, it joined No 23.

A longer line was still sought, and following negotiations with the Council at Eastbourne a new line, built to a 2-foot gauge, opened in 1953. An open-top car, No 3, was sent south with No 225, which was re-gauged. To replace the missing trams at Rhyl, a bogie toast-rack was built but was never as popular as the 'proper'-looking trams.

One cannot help wondering what would have hap-pened to these two tramways if Claude Lane and his Light Railway Transport League colleagues had been successful in their attempt to buy the L&CBER. As it was, Claude and his assistant, Allan Gardner, purchased a lot of equipment from the depot at Rhos-on-Sea in 1956 when the tramway closed. The Rhyl tramway lasted until September 1957, after which the line and equipment were removed and No 23 returned to Barnet. It was sold to Mr I. L. Cormack of the Scottish Tramway Museum Society, and in 1985 was donated to Brian Martin and the Merseyside Tramway Preservation Society.

Messrs Lane and Gardner went on to develop the trams at Eastbourne until, eventually, they had to vacate that site too. They secured the old railway trackbed between Seaton and Colyton in East Devon and the Seaton & District Electric Tramway was born. That was over 25 years ago, and the trams have continued to run ever since, many of them incorporating parts from the former L&CBER trams. On 23 May 1994 ownership of tram No 23 passed to Denis Butler, who has restored it to full working order.

Now in its new home and looking resplendent in a fresh coat of paint, No 23 is enjoying a new lease of life operating over a short length of track between its newly built depot and a maturing lilac tree. Denis poses with the tram he rode in as a child, never realising then that one day he would eventually own it. The tram is to be repainted to its original livery together with the logo 'Modern Tramways' fixed to each side. *Author*

THE YEAR 1996 could well have been described as the Year of the Tram. In March Project Tram 7 was launched in Llandudno to raise funds to recreate Llandudno & Colwyn Bay Electric Railway No 7 using a former Bournemouth tram body, found on the South Coast, which was of a similar type to those that operated on the L&CBER. The body is in North Wales currently being rebuilt, and it is hoped to eventually display and operate it. For more details, contact R. C. Best, Project Director, at 12 Y Felin, Conwy, Gwynedd, LL32 8LW.

In May 1996 Seaton tram No 6 was brought to Llandudno to take part in the annual Transport Extravaganza, which was held on the Bodafon Fields during the Bank Holiday weekend. A 300-yard length of rail had been laid on the former tramway trackbed over which it had been intended to operate the tram, but unfortunately the Railway Inspectorate would not sanction its use and it had to remain static. Nevertheless No 6 did attract a lot of attention.

History has a habit of repeating itself, and on 28 October Mostyn Estates announced that a planning application was to be made for the construction of a metre-gauge tramway to operate between The Pier and the Bodafon Fields at Craig-y-Don, serving the main shopping and tourist areas as well as coach and car parks. The tramway would link the town to a new visitor attraction to be located on the fields and also provide an environmentally friendly method of local transport.

The proposal envisages seven trams of the standard Parry People Mover flywheel electric heritage vehicles, 6.5 metres long and 2 metres wide (currently attracting the interest of a number of towns in the United Kingdom). The main benefits of the Parry system are its cost (a fraction of a conventional street tramway), the fact that the rails can be laid with the minimum of disruption to underground services, and the absence of unsightly overhead wires and vehicle emissions.

A hundred years ago Mostyn Estates were closely involved in negotiations over the construction of the original electric tramway, which ultimately contributed to the development and prosperity of the town. If current proposals pass the various planning stages, their tramway could be up and running for the millennium, exactly 102 years after the granting of the original Light Railway Order. For Llandudno, in transport terms at least, the wheel will have turned full circle.

Right Seaton & District Electric Tram No 6 seen at the Llandudno Transport Extravaganza on 5 May 1996. It is standing on part of the specially laid track on the former trackbed of the L&CBER. Several former tramway employees visited the event to see the tram and many stories about the old tramway were exchanged. This tram incorporates several parts taken from the full-size trams when they were scrapped in 1956, including top-deck seats and mesh from L&CB 8, as well as headlamps, gongs, bells and circuit breakers from other L&CB trams. *Author*

Left A model showing the proposed trams for the new Llandudno Street Tramway Ltd went on display on 28 October 1996. The promoter specified the old-style pattern of Parry People Mover, and the livery of yellow, green and red with white lining is in marked contrast to that of the Great Orme Tramway to avoid any comparison. *John Symons*

This index includes people and places mentioned in the main text and captions.

A55 Expressway 11, 60, 61, 65
Abergele Road 7, 10, 12, 14, 83, 120
Abbey Road 23, 121
Accrington Corporation Tramways 14, 31
'Alice in Wonderland' 8, 128
Arcadia Cinema, Colwyn Bay 91
Arcadia Theatre, Llandudno 19, 41
Astra Cinema, Colwyn Bay 63

Baguley, E. E. Ltd 16, 33, 69
Balfour, Alexander 14
BBC Variety Department 40
Bellamy, Joe 22
Benarth Road 50
Bird, Geoff 43, 75
Birmingham Corporation Tramways 3, 31, 78
Birmingham & Midland Motor Omnibus Co Ltd 16
Board School, Colwyn Bay 61
Board of Trade 9-11, 14
Bodafon Fields 7, 8, 16, 21, 22, 26, 42, 43, 45, 71, 102-5, 118, 131
Bodafon Road 101
Bournemouth Corporation Tramways/Transport 14, 16, 21, 22, 31, 32, 116
Broadway Hotel 39, 108
Brompton Avenue 7, 10, 12, 59-61, 87-9, 113
Bryn-y-Bia Road 7, 45, 46, 100-3
Butler, Denis 130
Butterworth, Walter 19, 71, 80, 120

Caley Promenade, Rhos-on-Sea 27, 58, 59, 89, 90
Campbell, P. & A. Ltd 123
Canvey Island 28
Carroll, Lewis 8
'Carmen Sylva' 38
Carmen Sylva Road 103, 106
Catlin Follies 41
Chadderton, 'Nat' 53
Challenge Trophy 79

Church Road 8, 54, 92
Church Walks 126
Clifton Road 35
Codman, Professor 7
Coed-Pellar Road 12, 63, 64
Colwyn Avenue 10
Colwyn Bay Council 10, 12, 14, 18, 19, 23, 64, 91, 122, 129
Colwyn Bay Cricket Club 55
Colwyn Crescent 22, 56
Conway Road, Colwyn Bay 8, 10, 12, 61-4, 70, 84, 86
Conway Road, Llandudno 8
Conway Suspension Bridge 39
Craigside 8, 22, 26, 42-4, 103, 116
Craig-y-Don 8, 12, 38, 43, 71, 103, 104, 107, 115, 131
Crosland-Taylor, W. J. 19
Crosville Motor Services Ltd 7, 8, 14-6, 19, 23, 37, 39-41, 46, 47, 65, 84-6, 101, 103, 108, 109, 121

Darwen Corporation Tramways 16, 31, 32, 69, 70
Deganwy 9
Deutsch, Oscar 63
Dudman, Stanley 120

Eastbourne 130
Ebenezer Mission Hall 68
Elisabeth, Queen of Roumania 38, 106
English Presbyterian Church 70, 111
Evans, Tom 113

Francis, J. Fred & Sons 10

Gardner, Allan J. V. 130
Glan-y-Mor Road 22, 23, 48-50, 96-8
Gloddaeth Avenue 8, 23, 35, 111
Gloddaeth Street 35, 37, 38, 108-11
Grand Theatre 19, 40, 41
Great Orme 7, 8
Great Orme Copper Mines 8, 127
Great Orme Railway 7, 126
Great Orme's Road 35
Green, Hughie 91
Greenfield Road 14, 66, 67
Groes Road 10

Halfway Station 7, 126
Hamilton, Walter G. 14, 19, 38, 50
Happy Valley 7, 128
Harris, Alf 21, 22
Hooson's Corner 10, 36
Horton, William 9, 10
Hughes, Cllr E. 22
Hughes, 'Farmer' Dick 21, 116, 118

Imperial Hotel 21, 118
Isle of Man Steam Packet Co Ltd 123
Isles, Eric 42
Ivy Street 14, 85

Johnson, Reg 78, 95
Johnson, Rene 22
Jones, Evan 21, 75
Jones, H. T. 19
Jones, John Glyn 21, 22, 66
Jones, William Arthur 85

Lane, Claude 129, 130
Larkman, Percy 119
Lawson, P. W. 78
Lawson, Roger 78
Leamington & Warwick Tramways 14, 33
Levis, Carroll 91
Light Railway Orders/Promoters (various) 9-11, 23, 131
Light Railway Transport League 80, 82, 97, 130
Little Orme 7, 10, 19, 42, 48, 54, 97
Little Orme Cafe 16, 47-9, 54, 99
Liverpool & North Wales Steamship Co Ltd 7, 123
Llandudno, proposed new tramway (1996) 131
Llandudno Council 9, 10, 14, 18, 19, 107, 126
Llandudno Museum 108
Llandudno Pier 123, 124, 131
Llandudno Town Depot (Crosville) 41
Llanerch Road East 59, 88
Lloyd Street 38

Maesgwyn Road 18, 21, 48, 51, 117
Marine Drive and Toll Gate/Road 9, 16, 21, 23, 52-4, 95, 96
Marine Road 63
Mersey Tunnel 69
Merseyside & North Wales Electricity Board 18, 19
Merseyside Tramway Preservation Society 130

Ministry of Transport 11, 14, 16-8, 23, 95
Morfa Road 22, 52
Morgan, Bob 3, 21, 22, 116, 118
Morris, M. K. 23, 114
Mostyn, The Hon E. M. L., JP 9
Mostyn Avenue 42, 105, 106
Mostyn Broadway 16, 18, 19, 39-41, 76, 77, 107, 118
Mostyn Estates 131
Mostyn Street 7, 16, 18, 19, 26, 37-9, 77, 108, 109
Mount Stewart Hotel 59, 90

Nall, Sir Joseph 14, 16, 19
Nant-y-Gamar Road 22, 42, 103, 104, 114
Nicholson, Jock 95
North Wales Silver Motors 14
North West Traffic Commissioners 19, 23
North Western Hotel 8, 21, 39, 76, 77, 80, 108, 118

Oakley, George 80
Odeon Cinema, Colwyn Bay 63
Odeon Cinema, Llandudno 35, 110
Old Colwyn 10-12, 14, 21, 67
Orme Point 9, 21, 22, 54, 94, 122
Owen, Cllr J. O. 21
Owen, Les 50, 88

Palladium Corner 7, 8, 18, 35-8, 81, 109, 110, 114
Parry People Mover 131
Peacock, John 23
Penmaen Head 10, 11, 86
Penrhyn Avenue 3, 8-10, 15, 22, 23, 54-7, 63, 91, 92, 94, 117, 121
Penrhyn Bay 14, 16-9, 48, 50, 51, 54, 75, 95, 97
Penrhyn Hill 10, 16, 21-3, 26, 27, 43, 46-9, 70, 80, 99-102
Penrhyn Isaf Road 98
Penrhynside 46, 49
Perril, Bill 12
Pitman, Herbert 17, 56
Poole & District Electric Traction Co 14, 33
Porter, John 64
'Project Tram 7' 131
Pugh, Emrys 83

Quarry Cottages 48, 97
Queen's Hotel 10, 11, 14
Queen's Road 106, 115

Rhos-on-Sea 8-11, 14, 27, 57, 78, 91
Rhos Depot 8, 22, 23, 27, 71-5, 93, 116, 117, 119, 120
Rhos Golf Club 9, 18, 22, 52, 53, 79, 97
Rhos Pier 90, 91
Rhos Playhouse 57
Rhyl 9, 22, 70, 129, 130
Richardson, Mr 22, 32
Roberts, Bill 96
Rolt, L. T. C. 21

St Beuno's Road 128
St David's Corner 21, 49, 50, 98
St John's Methodist Church 85
St Leonards (Hastings) 129
St Paul's Church, Colwyn Bay 14, 64, 66, 67, 83-5
St Paul's Church, Craig-y-Don 107
St Seriol 123, 125
St Silio/St Trillo 123, 125
St Tudno 7, 123, 124
Seaton & District Electric Tramway 130, 131
Sprout, Doris 114
Station Road 10, 12, 64
Sunderland Corporation Transport 19, 31

Talyllyn Railway 21
Taunton Electric Traction Co Ltd 33
Tramway Preservation Committee 21
Tudor Road 19, 77

Upper Mostyn Street 109

Victoria Station (Great Orme Railway) 126, 128
Von Donop, Lieut Col 10
Vroyd Amusement Park 129

West End 61-3, 87
West Parade 9, 10
West Shore 7, 8, 10, 12, 18, 19, 21, 34, 36, 111, 112, 119, 121
Whitehall Road 12, 89
Williams, Bobby 43
Woodlands Road West 12, 64
Woolley, F. A. 79
Woolley, J. E. 14, 21, 22, 40, 79, 82, 97, 116, 120